Neighbours from Hell?

English attitudes to the Welsh

Mike Park

y Lolfa

First impression: 2007
Reprint: 2014
© Copyright Text and Photographs: Mike Parker and Y Lolfa Cyf., 2007
© Copyright Original cartoons: Toby Driver

The publishers wish to acknowledge the financial support of
Cyngor Llyfrau Cymru

Cover photograph: Graham Hembrough
Cover design: Y Lolfa

ISBN: 0 86243 611 7
9780862436117

Published and printed in Wales by
Y Lolfa Cyf., Talybont, Ceredigion SY24 5HE
website www.ylolfa.com
e-mail ylolfa@ylolfa.com
tel. 01970 832 304
fax 832 782

*How can an elite of usurpers, aware of their mediocrity,
establish their privileges? By one means only: debasing the
colonised to exalt themselves, denying the title of humanity to
the natives, and defining them simply as absences of qualities
– animals, not humans. This does not prove hard to do, for the
system deprives them of everything.*

Jean-Paul Sartre

CONTENTS

PREFACE

When I write anything for publication or broadcast, I generally aim to fix in my mind's eye at least a vague picture of a person for whom I believe I am writing. Having chucked in my stuttering stand-up comedy career when I moved to rural mid Wales (there's not much of a stand-up circuit in the Dyfi valley), I don't have many opportunities these days to get such immediate feedback. At least with stand-up, I could see the punters and see whether I was entertaining them, provoking them, or just boring them rigid. No such luxury with the written word.

When I'm writing the *Rough Guide to Wales*, I picture a faintly bemused, but heartily enthusiastic, American tourist clopping around some castle or other. For my column in the *Big Issue Cymru*, the 'street paper' sold by homeless vendors, I envisage an urban reader in Cardiff, Swansea or Bangor, someone who's probably hoping to catch some art house movie before knocking up a Thai meal for their clever and trendy mates. For the ITV Wales travelogue programmes that I write and present (*Coast to Coast* and latterly *Great Welsh Roads*), I know all too well that many of the people tuned in are probably far more occupied with eating their tea, doing their homework, cutting their toenails, having a row, a cwtch, or just idly daydreaming, though, of course, I like to believe (and sod it, I *will* believe) that a sizeable number are watching in rapt attention and hanging on my every word.

Writing this book, however, has been very different. I have absolutely no mental image of who is likely to read it. I know who I'd like to read it, but that's not the same thing at all. I hope that it doesn't just fall into the hands of, shall we say, the usual suspects, people who already know all too well the savageness of English attitudes to all things Welsh and who look to this book only to confirm their already cast-iron certainties. As an English incomer into Wales, it is my fellow in-migrants that I'd most like to see clutching a copy. That's not to say that I want us to live our lives in the sackcloth of repentance, beating ourselves up and apologising for our English heritage to anyone who'll listen. But I do want English people moving to Wales, or who have been here a long time, to realise that to live here successfully is to commit one's self to this fierce and fantastic little country. And to remember that it is a different country.

This book is not a lengthy apology for being English. Although I had very little choice in the matter, I'm still proud to be English, and for very many reasons. It is a culture that has bequeathed a mountain of positive improvements to the world, from its eternally iconoclastic, rebellious elements to beauty and art that thrill you to the core. Any culture that could spit out Shakespeare and the Sex Pistols, William Blake and the Cadbury Flake, Old Peculier and the Ordnance Survey has to be given mucho credit. Not generally included in this long list, though, is England's not-so-benign ability to rule other countries. Yes, those countries might get railways, mines, punctuality and technology, but they are often left, stripped, confused and defenceless in a hostile world. There is the old saying that Wales was England's first colony, and likely to be its last. Plaid Cymru MP Adam Price put it beautifully in a recent interview: he was very fond of the real England; his problem was with the British Establishment. There is a world of difference between the two.

INTRODUCTION

*To recognise the separate existence of Wales and the Welsh
as a distinct people, with their own history and their own
language, involves for an English person a distinct movement of
conversion. For fifteen hundred years we have been pretending
that our Western neighbours are not there, or that if they are,
they are beneath our contempt, not worth our attention.*

Canon AM Allchin, in *Discovering Welshness*, 1992

Like most next-door neighbours, the Welsh and the
English have co-existed, sometimes amicably, often
not. Neighbourly grumbles and stereotypes between the two
nations have developed and dragged on for centuries, ever since
Offa's Dyke – that eighth-century equivalent of quick-growing
leylandii trees – was built.

Of course, these are not neighbours of equal size and
power. To stretch the analogy further, the English are akin
to a rich and powerful family in the Big House, while the
Welsh hunker down in their *bwthyn*, on the estate's western
edge. In many ways, the attitude of the English over the years
has mirrored this analogy, being characterised, at best, by a
pompous paternalism and, at worst, by outright condescension
and outrageous *Cymrophobia*. Mind you, there are some from
the rich family who have admired, and even yearned for, the
apparent simplicity and earthiness of life in the Welsh *bwthyn*.
There are many complicated strands to this neighbourly
relationship, strands that stretch back thousands of years, to
the dawn of *any* sense of nationhood on this small island.

The low-level niggling between England and Wales is a

recognisable feature of any two unequally-sized, adjoining cultures: you can easily see parallels in the relationship between the Basques and the Spanish (and French); the Czechs and Slovaks; Canada and the USA; New Zealand and Australia; Germany and Poland; the smaller ex-Soviet states and Russia, practically anywhere on our stroppy little planet. Likewise, the ways in which such grumbles manifest themselves are much the same now as they have ever been.

The idea for this book came when I was reading some snide aside about the Welsh language in one of the London Sunday broadsheet newspapers, something along the lines of, 'Welsh has no vowels and sounds like spitting.' It dawned on me that I'd heard and seen such comments many times before, when researching Welsh history, and that the same tired old clichés were passed down from generation to generation, like a particularly wearisome game of Chinese Whispers. Unfortunately, the people who write this kind of tosh usually think that they are the first to come up with such a pithy put-down; you can practically hear them howling with laughter at their own originality and wit. Writing this book has been my way of showing them for the intellectual retards that they generally are: inheritors of a long line of naked racism, rather than the purveyors of anything particularly useful, original or illuminating.

To that end, I've taken a variety of subject areas and attempted to dig deep into the well of comments made about them over the centuries. There are obvious flashpoints; the Welsh language has always proven to be something which English commentators feel particularly vehement in dismissing, but there are many less flagrant examples, too. Even the Welsh landscape, something marketed these days as the perfect antidote to urban English stresses, has, over the years, been on the sharp end of many withering put-downs from across the border, especially when it has given commentators an opportunity to conflate its perceived shortcomings with those of the Welsh people as a whole.

As can be seen throughout the text, some Welsh people themselves have not been averse to echoing the haughtiest put-downs of the English, and, where appropriate, I've included them. Not included here are the attitudes of the Welsh to England and the English – that, I suspect, is another book, for another day and another author. The bulk of the cross-border sniping that I've discussed in this book have come from the last few hundred years. English antipathy towards the Welsh, however, goes back an awful lot further – to times when the concepts of 'England' and 'Wales' had barely come into existence. This is a very long game.

For an overview of this early history, see Chapter 7.

Chapter 1

THIEVES AND TROLLS:
The Welsh Character

*The Welsh are cordially liked and heartily respected by all their
fellow-subjects, as a gallant and most gifted race. Year by year,
the English know them better, and year by year the English
like them more. There really is not a lingering trace of national
jealousy. Long ago, we fought our last fight with the Welsh, and
luckily for them we won it.*

Daily Telegraph editorial, 15 September 1867

Picture the scene. A Victorian children's nursery, the darling
offspring of the emergent English middle classes reciting
their times table by rote, in front of a starched-aproned
governess. All around them are the tools to educate the children
in the knowledge that they are the most blessed in the entire
world, and that their superiority knows no bounds. A map of
the world is splashed in Empire Red. F is for Fuzzy-Wuzzy,
states the alphabet chart, over a grotesque cartoon image of an
African man. Everyone else not fortunate enough to be born
English, is caricatured, ridiculed and scorned. All together
now, children, let us recite our favourite nursery rhyme:

Taffy was a Welshman, Taffy was a thief,
Taffy came to my house and stole a leg of beef.
I went to Taffy's house, Taffy was in bed,
I picked up a poker and hit him on the head.

You've got to hand it to the Victorians. Within just a couple of
childish rhyming couplets, they successfully imparted a raft of

violent prejudice into the heads of their little ones. Taffy will break into your house, nick your goods, spends most of his time indulgently scratching his arse, in bed, and is really only worth bothering about as target practice. Job well done.

Of course, in these PC times, reciting such a rhyme in a schoolyard would probably bring an army of social workers on to the scene within minutes. The words may well be inadmissible, but the sentiment lingers like a bad smell. Ask many English people what their perceptions of the Welsh character are, and the same old qualities keep rearing their tired old heads: the Welsh are sly, cunning, unentrepreneurial, unfriendly, secretive, sentimental, and lazy. No surprise that, in 2001, North Wales won a BBC Radio Five Live phone-in competition to find the UK's least friendly place, edging out London – that cheerful, happy-go-lucky metropolis – in the final stages. Almost everyone who voted for North Wales came out with one of the old 'I went into a pub and they all started speaking Welsh' diatribes as proof of the region's lack of courtesy.

The strangest aspect to this widespread distaste for all things Cymreig is how broad-based it is. Even those who would sooner lop off a limb than admit to being racist are more than happy to pitch in with their tuppence-worth. When I finally decided to move to rural Wales from the English West Midlands, acquaintances of the most right-on variety, *Guardian*-readers to the core, thought nothing of trotting out every in-breeding, sheep-shagging, language-switching, house-burning cliché in the book. These are people who've marched and signed petitions for downtrodden folk in Nicaragua, South Africa, Ireland, Indonesia, Australia, the Balkans, Iraq, Palestine and whichever part of our petulant little planet was kicking off at the time. They buy coffee that doesn't oppress anyone, fill their homes with eco-friendly world knick-knacks and make loud noises about their loathing of English imperialism. But, somehow, one people escapes their gimlet gaze of well-meaning solidarity, and it is the one geographically closest to them, the Welsh. As Dai Smith put it, 'Wales, unlike Ireland, has never quite caught the English Left's ear. It is as if the propinquity and sustained ambiguity of Wales is too much, too close, to grasp for those who can only hear distant trumpets.' In other words, the Welsh are still fair game.

The inescapable truth of this came home to me on many an occasion during my attempt at a stand-up comedy career, in the late 1990s – the career itself probably more laughable than most of my material. As a youngster in the super Seventies, I well recall how the Irish were the favourite comedy racial grouping of the moment. Barely any Saturday night light entertainment TV show passed without some gags about thick Paddies and the like, usually from some gurning gargoyle in a ruffled shirt and velvet bow-tie. The rise of so-called alternative comedy in the shoulder-padded 1980s put paid to the Irish gags, as well as the ones taking the piss out of black people and Asians (another staple of seventies' comedians). Somehow, the Welsh came to replace them all as the racial grouping you could still rip to bits without ruining your appetite and none more so than on the supposedly 'alternative' stand-up circuit. I lost count of the misanthropic young men I witnessed, who, when their act was struggling and the audience were starting to look a little too attentively at their nails, would dip into the bottom of the comedy barrel and chuck out a few disparaging comments about the Welsh. You could hardly blame them, I guess: it was almost guaranteed to raise a laugh, and even a cheer, amongst the young sophisticates of urban England.

If you're playing to an English audience, slagging off the Welsh is a sure-fire winner almost every time, and it's no surprise that so many loud-mouthed desperadoes on TV have resorted to it. The irony there, of course, is that the TV programmes are almost always broadcast beyond England, as well, but that seems to get forgotten by the contributors (let alone the schedulers). Of them all, Jeremy Clarkson is the one that has, perhaps, been the most inventive in his anti-Welsh posturing, best seen in his eponymous chat show, when he cut Wales off a plastic relief map of Britain and set fire to it in a microwave.

Clarkson is a bit of a hero to many a grumpy, middle-aged, English Viagra-addict in saggy jeans, and has spawned a plethora of media Mini Mes, to cuss on cue, though rarely with any of the aplomb of the original. One of his underlings on *Top Gear*, James May, has evidently decided to take pot-shots at much the same targets as his mentor, in the hope that it will bring him the same lucrative newspaper columns and TV contracts. Thus it was that he had a dig at bilingual road signs in Wales, one of the easiest targets for someone with such a limp aim:

> *Fair enough if a bunch of pasty-faced ginger separatists insist*
> *on conversing in their native tongue, that's their lookout,*
> *but for the rest of us it's baffling and even dangerous... The*
> *impression is that some nationalists have loaded a blunderbuss*
> *with consonants and then rampaged around the land firing*
> *indiscriminately at the road furniture.*
>
> Daily Telegraph

I'm sure Mr Clarkson was very proud of him. But he still hasn't got a column in a Sunday newspaper.

Edwardian Values

To come back to the Victorians and Edwardians; the nineteenth and early twentieth centuries were a period in which Cymrophobia ran rampant through the English establishment, mirroring that same establishment's cast-iron surety in its own grand, unshakeable rectitude and power. Pompous, sweeping editorials were the stuff of the London press, while railway station bookstands were packed with snide little tuppenny works, belittling anyone and everyone not fortunate enough to be born middle-class and English.

This period is littered with characters that excelled in sucking up to the establishment, even, at times, at the expense of their own heritage. One particularly interesting example was Arthur Tysilio Johnson (1873-1956), an English-raised writer of Welsh extraction and one of the more obvious manifestations of the

Daio Jenkins from the Rhondda
Look You !.

The diabolical, black-faced miner. An Edwardian postcard which would surely send shivers down spines in the Home Counties.

By permission of the National Library of Wales

phenomenon of Dic Siôn Dafydd, that fictional Welsh arse-licker, who cements his credentials in England by becoming more English than the English. Johnson's speciality was dry and distinctly patrician books about horticultural and angling matters. Like many before and since, he was quite happy to play on a kind of stage Welshness, while firmly allying himself with some of the nastiest anti-Welsh, anti working-class sentiment of the time, thus securing for himself the best of both worlds in Edwardian England. His crowning glory in this field came in the shape of his 1910 book, *The Perfidious Welshman*, which contained the following gems:

> *Keep Taffy at arm's length, or he will take liberties, and become familiar.*
>
> *Few people can tell a lie to your face with such perfect composure as a Welshman.*
>
> *No people were ever less fitter to call a country their own and themselves a nation than the Welsh.*
>
> *Wales has no great women of good repute.*
>
> *To anyone who does not know the shallow transparency of the average Welsh mind, its utter want of ballast and lack of independence, the humbug with which the Welsh Member of Parliament feeds his herd of ignorant voters is almost beyond comprehension.*

He concluded his tedious tirade with words of advice, both to Welsh people and English. To the Welsh, he wrote, 'Anglicize yourself as speedily as you can. It will never be possible for you to be equal to an Englishman, but you make him your ideal and you may realise the misfortune of having been born Welsh. Forget your language as quickly as you can. It is vulgar to use it in decent society. Never mention your own country or its history more often than you can help.'

To the cast of admiring Englishmen whom Johnson doubtless pictured as he poured out his bile he wrote: 'never allow your children to be contaminated by the manners of Welsh children. Avoid the Welsh language as you would sin. Do not have a Welsh servant who is walking out with a young man. She can seldom be doing that and remain pure... Never employ a Welshman if you can help it, for he will not only be dishonest, but he will slander you all over the countryside... Taffy is a low-bred mongrel of Mongolian origin.'

This combination of smart-arse quip covering outright bigotry was a particular favourite of the Edwardians, in that strange Victorian hangover period that lasted up to the outbreak of World War I. Wales and the Welsh were an especially hot target of the time, largely due to the national prominence of

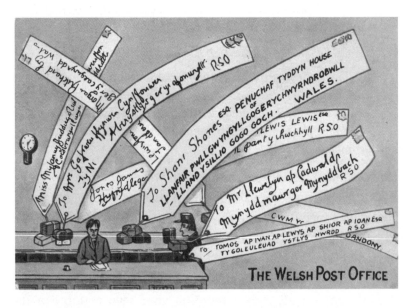

A favourite souvenir postcard of the Edwardian era. The joke was so funny, it was repeated *ad nauseam* on a stack of similar cards from the same era.

By permission of the National Library of Wales

David Lloyd George, wily Liberal politician, MP for Caernarfon and soon-to-be British Prime Minister. For many of the English political class, Lloyd George was the only true Cymro they had ever come across, and so every one of his strange foibles – his slipperiness, rhetoric and political expediency – was assumed to be a characteristic of the whole Welsh nation, rather than merely the personality traits of a deeply ambitious country solicitor. In many ways, Lloyd George served as a lightning conductor for anti-Welsh sentiment that has continued to this day, as will be seen later in the chapter.

One of the most notorious protagonists of the written snobbery of the Lloyd George age was Yorkshire journalist, publisher and poet, T W H Crosland, whose extreme right-wing version of a romanticized English nationalism was usually expressed through his virulent put-downs of other races and nations. To that end, he was a regular contributor to the viciously anti-Semitic journal, *Plain English*. Like most bullies, he also took great delight in picking on weaker neighbours, penning books and poems that particularly vilified the Scots, the Irish and the Welsh. His anti-Welsh tirade was best seen in his 1912 book, *Taffy was a Welshman*:

> *The fact is that Wales is a little land, and the Welsh are a little people, with little intellects and little views.*

> *Considered as a spectacle pure and simple, an Eisteddfod is a pitiful and almost squalid affair.*

> *It was Offa who built a dyke to separate Wales from England, and we are inclined to think that Offa was a man of sense and discernment.*

And, sounding strangely like the inspiration for *The Sunday Times's* A A Gill:

> *It is time we remembered that England is our messuage and*

demesne... and that Englishmen were born to rule and not be ruled, and least of all to be ruled by a bumptious, snuffling, flighty, tiresome, fifth-rate bunch of barbarians like the Welsh.

The nineteenth and early twentieth centuries were, perhaps, the zenith of acceptable sneering at Wales as a nation, its native language and the character of its citizens. But it wasn't just the English participating in the sport; like Arthur Tysilio Johnson, above, there was always a steady supply of Welsh people, too, playing the game. George Thomas, erstwhile Secretary of State for Wales, Speaker of the House of Commons and later Lord Thomas of Tonypandy, is seen by many as a later twentieth-century version of this unappealing phenomenon. Although Thomas was more than happy to play on his Valleys Welshness when it suited him, his strident denunciation of language campaigners, Plaid Cymru and anyone who dared to see Wales

More of the same from those wacky Edwardians.

By permission of the National Library of Wales

as a nation rather than as a convenient cultural badge, left a particularly nasty taste in the mouth. A recent release of Cabinet papers showed that the depth of his paranoia; when he was Secretary of State for Wales in the late 1960s, he even wrote (by hand, so that none of his officials would see) to the Prime Minister, Harold Wilson, expressing concerns that the Prince of Wales was sounding way too Welsh Nationalist for comfort, and could he, the PM, have a quiet word with Her Majesty, and ask her to calm her lad down a bit? When you start seeing Prince Charles as a rabid Nat, then you really do need to have a lie-down in a darkened room. The late Cledwyn Hughes, Labour MP for Anglesey, recounted how George Thomas had rung him to gloat over the four-to-one defeat of the devolution proposals in Wales in 1979. Hughes pointed out that, as Speaker of the House, Thomas was supposed to be entirely impartial. 'Oh, yes,' he replied, 'I am entirely impartial – but, on this issue, I know on which side I am impartial.'

Despite his red-hot Rhondda socialism (or so he liked to portray it), George Thomas was never happier than when surrounded in luxuriant finery by the trappings of the Westminster elite. Since his death, it has been revealed by his fellow south Welsh Labour MP, Leo Abse, that Thomas was a deeply unsettled, closet homosexual, who spent most of his adult life locked into a cycle of self-loathing for his sexual attraction towards men, before it finally became too much for him, at which point he'd engage in some furtive grapple in the back seats of a Soho porn cinema, which would quickly propel him back into the virulently self-loathing phase once again. It's not beyond reason to see the same monotonous streak of loathing towards his own culture running through his life and pronouncements.

'A Country Entirely Populated by Perverts'

And so to sex. The great totem, the great leveller of all time works its age-old magic in this strange relationship, too. Much to the annoyance of the English, the Welsh, despite (or perhaps because of) their chapel-going, hymn-singing ways, enjoy something of a highly-sexed reputation. Welsh characters in popular British TV series, from Ruth Madoc's Gladys in *Hi-de-Hi* to *Little Britain*'s Dafydd, are almost always gagging for it. Cymru is a lusty land, and the neighbours, pursing their lips disapprovingly from behind twitching net curtains, are, frankly, a mite jealous.

'Want of chastity is the giant sin of Wales,' opined the Reverend L H Davies, of Troed-yr-Aur, in Ceredigion, in the notorious Blue Books, the National Education Report of 1847. He went on to describe, in very well-observed detail, just what he meant:

> *[the young people] often meet at evening schools in private houses for the preparation of the pwnc, and this frequently leads to immoralities between the young persons of both sexes, who frequently spend the night afterwards in the hay lofts together. So prevalent is the want of chastity amongst the females, that, although I promised to return the marriage fee to all couples whose first child should be born after nine months from the marriage, only one in six years entitled themselves to claim it. Most of them were in the family-way...*

It was the repeated sexual insinuations in the Blue Books that most ignited its controversy. In every corner of the country, the inspectors reported that they found 'fornication and immorality' to be 'rife' and they spared no innuendo in passing on this finding, for all the difference it made to a report on education. Not only were the Welsh too randy for their own good, but the

"Damn it Gareth, we agreed - no ex-girlfriends invited."

Report also claimed that they suffered from 'aroused passion' and 'peculiar excitability', and that their 'reasoning powers are less developed' than those of the English. Bombastic conclusions about the Welsh language were one thing, but repeated snide nods to the perceived immorality of the Welsh transformed the report into one of the nastiest, meanest government documents ever produced – and that's really saying something. There was also the incontrovertible feeling that the conclusion of the report – that the Welsh were almost sub-human, and their language must be exterminated – was decided upon long before one single shred of evidence had been gathered, and that the people called upon to give evidence to the three monoglot English Commissioners were chosen in order to back this up. The Reverend Davies quoted above was one of two hundred and thirty-two Anglican priests interviewed by the three English

Commissioners, against just seventy-nine Nonconformist ministers – and that in a country where around eighty percent of the population attended Nonconformist chapels. Also hugely over-represented in giving evidence to the Commissioners were the Anglo-Welsh aristocracy, whose loathing of their poorer, monoglot Welsh neighbours was allowed free reign. It makes the gathering of intelligence to back Tony Blair's war in Iraq look like a masterstroke of diplomatic reasoning.

The earthy sensuality of Wales and her inhabitants has for long both fascinated and appalled the English, and none more so than its gentry and royalty, who, ordinarily, try to have as little to do with the place as possible. Rumours have persisted for four hundred years that the Virgin Queen, Elizabeth I, spirited herself away into the hills near Llangollen in order to give birth to a bastard child. Henry I impregnated the lovely Nest, the 'Helen of Wales', Charles II made whoopee with Lucy Walter, the 'Rhosmarket Siren', and it is thought that, while his heavily pregnant wife was languishing in the newly-built Caernarfon Castle, Edward I himself got to know at least one local female subject rather better than loyalty dictated.

Where the royals led, the officer class of Olde England was just behind, britches loosened in eager readiness. Never underestimate the depth of an Englishman's urge for something more primal, more basic than the elaborate lacework of middle-class, Protestant respectability that is his apparent birthright. Countless stories survive of nineteenth-century English officers running riot in the Colonies, their suburban strait jackets (and all other garments) evaporating in the heat of the African or Indian sun and the dusky loveliness of the natives. It was, as is nearly always claimed to be the case with bullies and rapists, never their fault. They were provoked, tempted beyond endurance, M'lud, by the wanton ways of these primitive

A 1964 report into the surprisingly liberal sexual mores of mining communities produced a few predictable pops. This cartoon by Stanley Franklin from the *Daily Mirror* has a particularly animalistic bunch of Welsh miners hurling ammunition at the report's author.

people – people, it would also generally be added, who have been unenlightened by the bromide of Christianity. They were, in short, asking for it, and, by George, they got it.

Although Wales has never offered the requisite temperatures for such shenanigans, what applied in the Raj had echoes in the attitudes that drifted across Offa's Dyke. The same sounds of prurient fascination, dressed up as haughty disapproval, have often been applied to the Welsh. An early English guide book (1821) to Aberystwyth noted, 'The lower classes here, as in many other parts of Wales, indiscriminately dress and undress on the sands, and pay very little distinction to their sex,' absolutely guaranteeing a steady stream of visitors, eager to witness the phenomenon, while tutting indignantly. The same tendency for locals to bathe naked was noted in Llandudno as late as the 1850s, causing scandal and raised pulses in pretty much equal measure. Such notoriety was surely a far better advert for the towns than any number of exhortations to enjoy the stiff sea breeze.

As the British Empire shrank to a few distant lumps of rock, Wales' erotic reputation survived intact. According to 2002's huge ICM/Observer poll of Britain's sexual statistics, the Welsh have significantly more sexual partners than those in any other part of the UK – more than twice as many in an average lifetime than folk from Yorkshire. Eckythump! As ever, the results provoked a predictable flurry of eyebrow-raising and innuendo in Wales' direction. I lost count of the number of jokes about just how many of the Welsh average total of sexual partners was accounted for by livestock, rather than fellow human beings. But there was a definite strain of jealousy creeping into the sneers, and even a grudging respect. Hinting at sexual extravagance might have caused outrage and disgust in the mid 1800s, but in the shagtastic twenty-first century, it's a certificate of honour. As Dylan Thomas, that great stage Welshman, playing to the gallery, had it: 'The more I know about Wales, the more I am aware that I live in a country entirely populated by perverts.' And if anyone could spot a fellow perv at forty paces, it's Dylan.

'The Devil Understands Welsh'

Inherent in the snooty disapproval of anything pertaining to matters sexual is a darker suspicion, and it is one that has surfaced reliably and regularly as the English contemplate their nearest neighbours. It is, quite simply, that there is something depraved and godless in Wales; that, for all its surface piety and religiosity, the hills are steeped in pagan insouciance and libidos running rampant. 'The Welsh are Christian in name only; they are barbarians,' sniffed the Archbishop of Canterbury, way back in 1159. A seventeenth-century English MP described the Welsh as, 'Devil worshippers, living like thieves and robbers in the mountains, the most base, peasantly, perfidious people in the World.' Shakespeare's Hotspur, in Henry IV, Part 1, states baldly, 'Now I perceive the Devil understands Welsh.' The *Sunday Times* journalist, A A Gill's much-vaunted 1998 observation that the Welsh are 'stunted, bigoted, dark, ugly, pugnacious little

"The Beatles, Doddy, Jimmy Tarbuck, Cilla Black — I think we're in for a charity show, look you!"

Cartoon by Jak (Raymond Jackson). The campaign against the flooding of the Tryweryn valley in Meirionydd became something of a cause célèbre on both sides, and it featured frequently in newspaper cartoons. In this one, published in the *London Evening Standard* of October 1965, the official delegation from Liverpool is arriving to open the new reservoir, watched from afar by disgruntled locals (or "taffies" as they surprisingly call themselves on one placard). Shortcuts indicate that the group is Welsh, most notably the fact that one of them is a witch on a broomstick, playing straight into an old, deep suspicion held by the English about their neighbours. Just in case you were in any doubt about her nationality, she ends her sentence with the proverbial 'look you', another favourite shtick of English clichés.

By permission of the *Daily Express*.

trolls', alluded to many of the same base characteristics.

The long-held idea that Wales is somehow a hotter bed of lust than its near neighbour is underpinned by many suspicions as to the supposed paganism of the Welsh. Two millennia of Christian propaganda have ensured that most people remain cheerfully ignorant of the differences between heathens, pagans, witches and Satanists. Everything, from the warty witches of children's fairy stories and pantomimes to church wall paintings and ecclesiastical art, has been used to suggest that anyone subscribing to a pre-Christian belief system is in bed with the Devil himself. In these islands, pre-Christian belief systems were based on an understanding of the land and its spirits, together with a profound knowledge of natural phenomena such as astronomy, herbalism and the cycle of the seasons.

It is certainly true that genuine pagan practice has never been fully extirpated in Wales. Even when the chapels were at their most packed and the rousing hymns rent the air, each village and community had its roster of wise women (and men), witches by any other name, to whom everyone would flock in times of need or seeking a remedy. Still surviving, especially in the remoter corners of Wales, is a number of old family witchcraft traditions, where secrets have been passed down through the generations, over many centuries. It's not hard to see why such things have endured better in rural Wales than in most parts of England. Pagan beliefs (the word itself simply comes from the Latin *pagus*, a rural dweller) are land-based, and the Welsh are far more defined by their land and landscape than those across the border. Even looking at the history of the Christian church in Wales, it is obvious that many of the older beliefs (and, for that matter, places of worship) were cannily appropriated by the emerging new religion, in a far greater way than happened in the English church. Chastity, for instance, was never demanded of the early Welsh priests, in direct contrast to the Augustine precepts in England. God and no sex? A contradiction in terms!

To show the Welsh as godless and heathen also meant that they were, therefore, out of the loop when it came to the apparent benefits of Christianity. Heaven, English people were frequently reassured, was a place reserved for them, an eternal game of cricket on a celestial village green. In his *Merry Tales*, sixteenth-century English poet John Skelton created the image of St Peter managing to get shot of the Welsh from Heaven by shouting, 'Roasted cheese,' at the Pearly Gates, thus tempting them out and leaving the chosen ones to enjoy their well-deserved eternal rest.

Today, paganism, like upfront sexuality, is a far more accepted and even venerated concept, as society gradually overturns its deep-seated hang-ups inherited from centuries of aggressive, muscular Christianity. Indeed, it could be said that paganism has become trendy, mixed in, as it so often is, with a whole plethora of New Age pick'n'mix beliefs: a bit of Native American shamanism sprinkled with some Eastern mysticism or transcendental meditation, a dash of astrology, some misty Celtic mumbling and topped with a few crystals, tarot cards, self-help books and a veneer of Harry Potter or Buffy the Vampire Slayer. There are inordinate numbers of recent English émigrés to Wales who loosely subscribe to this hotchpotch of beliefs, as can be seen by the profusion of re-birthing retreats, New Age camps, vegan B&Bs and the like across the country. Their faith, like so much of their lives, is often woolly and unspecific, and the greatest irony of all is that, amongst the influences cherry-picked from marginalised cultures across the globe, the one that they copiously ignore is the one on their own doorstep. Real Welsh paganism, rooted deep in the mud and the rain and the rock, is far too difficult and dirty for such dilettante attitudes.

Economist John Maynard Keynes unconsciously echoed many previous commentators (and foreshadowed many more), when he tried, in 1933, to pin down the elusive character of David Lloyd George, the former British Prime Minister, who hailed from the heartland of *y fro Gymraeg* in Caernarfonshire:

> *How can I convey to the reader, who does not know him, any just impression of this extraordinary figure of our time, this siren, this goat-footed bard, this half-human visitor to our age from the hag-ridden magic and enchanted woods of Celtic antiquity?*

Once again, there is a subliminal comparison going on between the rational and reasonable Englishman and the quixotic, animalistic Welshman. From the English point of view, it's a comparison that, like the report of the Blue Books, always has

THE SAXON: "AM I ON THE RIGHT WAY FOR BANGOR?"

THE WELSH DEACON: "ISS, SURE. GO ROUND THE CHWITH AN' TROI I LAWR LON LLECHI-LLWYDION TILL YOU COME AT TY MARI TOMOS, AN' THEN CROSS AFON TROBWLL, AN' —— " (EXIT SAXON.)

By permission of the National Library of Wales

a set outcome, before any of the evidence is actually gathered; namely, that the Welshman is inferior, one of the 'barefoot rascals' (the English parliament's description of Owain Glyndŵr's troops) who is best ignored or, if he becomes a little too vociferous, cruelly quashed.

'The Welsh Windbag'

Lloyd George was also the first Welsh politician to gain the epithet of The Welsh Windbag, a nickname that has been applied with varying degrees of adhesion to a few politicians (and others). A cursory internet search shows that the title has been granted, at some time or other, to a motley crew that includes Dylan Thomas, Anthony Hopkins, Tom Jones, Harry Secombe, Archbishop of Canterbury Dr Rowan Williams, actor John Rhys-Davies, John Humphreys, footballer Craig Bellamy, Eurovision singer James Fox and Swansea City FC director Mike Lewis. The phrase even makes it into Dutch (*de Welshe praatjesmaker*), which most certainly does lose something in translation.

The term Welsh Windbag is, however, most stubbornly associated these days with Neil Kinnock, erstwhile leader of the Labour party (1983-92), EU Commissioner and latter-day Baron Kinnock of Bedwellty. In the case of many of the people listed above, the phrase has just been a lazy sideswipe, but for Kinnock it became an albatross. Now, there are many good reasons to distrust Neil Kinnock, but his Welshness is not one of them.

It is widely accepted by many commentators that Kinnock's particular brand of Valleys verbosity alienated sufficient English voters to ensure John Major's shock re-election in 1992. We forget now how close it was: the Conservatives would have been denied an overall majority if they had lost only eleven more seats – and the total of the eleven lowest Tory majorities in that election was a tiny 2466 votes. Had just 1234 Middle Englanders – and residents of the Vale of Glamorgan, whose Tory MP had the slimmest majority of all, 19 votes – cast their ballots differently, the Tories could have been toast a full five years earlier. The 'Kinnock Factor' accounted for a great deal more than 1234 lost votes, and all thanks to the London papers wasting no time in trashing Kinnock, for his nationality as much as for his manifesto. *The Sun*, particularly, constantly referred to him as the Welsh Windbag throughout the campaign (and continues to do so to this day). Although Kinnock was the third Labour leader in a row (after 'Sunny' Jim Callaghan and Michael Foot) who represented a south Welsh constituency, he was the only one truly steeped in the culture of the area, and, most importantly to sensitive English ears, he was the only one who looked and *sounded* Welsh. It was a huge deciding factor. As the late (and very lamented) comedian Linda Smith put it to Kinnock, when he was chairing an episode of the BBC topical quiz, *Have I Got News for You?*, 'In 1992, do you think you'd have won if, instead of campaigning, you'd just pissed off on holiday for three weeks? Just gone away, kept your gob off the telly, and maybe replaced yourself with a lovely little kitten or something?'

I canvassed for the Labour party in the 1992 election, in some of Birmingham's more curtain-twitching suburbs, and lost count of how many people said, 'I'm not voting for that Welsh whinger/windbag/wanker/waste of space,' before triumphantly slamming the door in my face. More often than not, such a response came on the neatly-clipped front paths of countless 1930's semis, usually from middle-aged men in cardigans with elbow patches, who'd been called to talk to me by their wives. If they ever bothered to tell me any other reasons for not voting

Labour, it was usually along the lines of 'Because you lot will let more blacks in.' Lovely people. One bloke actually chased me down the street, hollering, 'You're just Communists, you lot; you're bastards, go back to Russia.' A neighbour informed me that this was the headmaster of the local primary school.

The Welsh Windbag is a truly revealing term, for it implies not just a fondness for words, but a massive overuse of them, almost to the point where they become useless. This, too, is part of the age-old English stereotype of the Welsh, and usually implies not just excessive loquaciousness but a high level of smugness (often combined with utter ineptitude) within it. It's a very old theme. When quiz show dominatrix Anne Robinson made her much chewed-over remarks about the Welsh, in the BBC show *Room 101*, she resuscitated many old chestnuts, including the statement that 'The Welsh are always so pleased with themselves.' Being called so pleased with yourself by Anne Robinson is like having William Hague point out that you're going a bit thin on top.

Even William Shakespeare wasn't immune to a bit of cheap ethnic stereotyping. His comical captain Fluellen (a deliberate mishearing of the name Llewellyn), in *Henry V*, is perhaps the first Welsh Windbag in English literature. Never content to use five words when fifty will do, Fluellen trips over his words, scatters 'look you' through every long-winded utterance and, in a scene often cut in these more politically correct times, force feeds an uppity English officer with leeks (geddit?!) for perceived slights on his nationhood. Like the character in the BBC Asian sketch show, *Goodness Gracious Me*, who insists that anything good is Indian, Fluellen cannot resist an opportunity to point out that anything noble or classical has a finer equivalent in Wales. *Henry V* is Shakespeare-meets-Benny Hill in places, for the roster of crude stereotypes (not just hapless, touchy Fluellen, but Jams, the dour Scottish officer, MacMorris, the belligerent Irish one, and various bewildered, conniving Frenchmen into the bargain) is unrelenting throughout.

This idea that the Welsh are smug and self-satisfied runs rich through centuries of English comment. A hundred years before Anne Robinson's spilled spleen, essayist and poet Sir Walter Raleigh (not to be confused with Queen Elizabeth I's favourite of the same name) harrumphed, 'The Welsh are so damned Welsh it sounds like affectation,' a bizarre sentiment that you cannot imagine being said about any other nationality. The same idea was expressed a further century before, when an English traveller in northern Wales, one E B, made the acid comment that, 'Nothing can be imagined so troublesome as a Welshman possessed with the spirit of genealogy.' As is so often the case, though, you can quite easily detect a vein of raw envy running through such pronouncements: the English, after all, are something of a mongrel race. They do not like the fact that their near neighbours are far more settled on their land, or that they have been there for millennia.

'An Unenterprising People'

If the Welsh are seen by the English as being appreciably different in the great themes of life, such as sex, religion, class and politics, so it is with their attitude to another main plank of life: money. For centuries, the English have caricatured the Welsh as lacking in entrepreneurship, ambition and the killer thrust of commerce – a country, '...inhabited by an unenterprising people,' as an 1866 editorial in *The Times* had it. In 2003, the then Home Secretary, David Blunkett, felt able to congratulate world champion hurdler, Colin Jackson that he had succeeded 'despite being Welsh' (in a speech at an anti-racism conference, of all places!).

Memorial tablet, Tenby. Inscription reads: 'This tablet was raised by a few Ladies & Gentlemen, to preserve from oblivion the Memory of PEGGY DAVIES. Bathing woman for 42 years to the ladies who visited TENBY; Her good humour, respectful attention, & gratitude; made her employers – Friends; On the 29th of September 1809, in the Water, She was seized with Apoplexy, & expired, Aged 82.'
Behind the sentimental language lurks a starker picture of a local lady scraping and bowing to wealthy visitors for over four decades, before dying in a cold autumn sea decades after she should have been able to retire.
Photo: author

To many people, the often more modest ambitions of the Welsh could be seen as something of a virtue, not a vice. A piece in the *New York Times* in 1889 compared the contributions of the Irish, Scots and Welsh to the infant USA, and drew some prescient conclusions: '...the Welsh, modest, unassuming, with no desire to shine, or to challenge the pretensions of their brothers, with quiet industry and unaffected dignity, have worked and laboured in various fields, winning for themselves neither fame nor fortune, but a quiet safe place and secure in the respect and confidence of their fellow men.'

The idea of the Welsh as an unenterprising people has been stated so often, and in so many ways, that it has, even without necessarily being true, become something of a truism. Foreshadowing a more recent quotation by George W Bush, the 1950s boss of the Steel Company of Wales, Fred Cartwright, said, in an after-dinner speech to Swansea businessmen, that he'd looked in an English-Welsh dictionary and was perturbed to see that there was no Welsh word for entrepreneur. In reply, someone asked him what, then, was the English word for this; a point he singularly failed to understand.

Certainly, by the rapacious standards of Anglo-American capitalism, Welsh culture and the people it produces seem to lack the no-holds-barred instinct that places material wealth as the sole objective in life. In the current climate, where the pure capitalist model of rampant consumerism is blasted at us from all sides as the one to which we should all aspire, the traditional Welsh way may indeed seem to be unenterprising. For very many people, though, this is a hugely welcome reminder of other ways of being; that money isn't everything, and that attributes such as strength of community and egalitarianism, creativity and spirituality matter more, even if they don't appear on a balance sheet.

The idea that the Welsh are lacking in enterprise first took hold in a big way during the Industrial Revolution. As layers of valuable minerals were discovered in the Welsh landscape, it was nearly always left to English capitalists to steam in and set up the huge-scale production to exploit these minerals as comprehensively as possible. As has happened since the year dot, wealth begat wealth, and it was the already wealthy (almost invariably English 'new money' or the Anglo-Welsh aristocracy) who had the available resources of land, money and political power to build and run the mines and quarries. It's impossible to say how the south Wales coal industry, for instance, would have been managed, had it been run by the Welsh themselves, but it's probably safe to say that the merciless rape of the land and its sudden abandonment (together with the often brutal conditions laid on the workers and their families) would have been very different in local hands. If that's unentrepreneurial, count me in.

The Welsh, indeed, often have a slightly strange relationship with money. It's quite normal to hear Welsh speakers, deep in conversation, quote costs in English, as if *yr iaith y nefoedd* (the language of the heavens) should not be sullied by such squalid consideration as prices and cash. There's also the very different approach Welsh businesses often take to promoting themselves, something with which many English people can't quite cope. My local estate agent, for instance, works a very reasonable Monday to Friday regimen, with an hour off for lunch and no weekend opening. To incomers, used to pushy Nigels selling property 24/7, such apparent lackadaisical business acumen is nigh-on unforgivable, and one of the most common complaints you'll hear amongst the English middle-classes hereabouts is a tetchy, 'I mean, really, do they want to sell houses, or not?' They say they want to move somewhere with a slower pace of life, but then fail utterly to appreciate what that means, if and when it jars with what they're used to back in Surbiton or Sale. Such incomers reach boiling points of indignation when confronted with the traditional Welsh way of doing business, which is often much less formal and – inevitably in tight-knit rural communities – largely based on old networks of friends and family, and is not conducted strictly by the book.

But there is real enterprise in Welsh culture, too. It's different from the kind traditionally practised across the border, but it is no less imaginative or adventurous – especially when you consider the harsher economic conditions in which it is often rooted. Take the retail trade, for example. The great London department stores (D H Evans, Peter Jones, John Lewis, Dickens and Jones, Owen Owen) were all founded by Welsh entrepreneurs, who had built up their trade over centuries, from Ceredigion and Carmarthenshire and other points of mid and west Wales to the markets of south-east England and the Midlands. The first waves were the drovers, taking hundreds of cattle in huge convoys across Wales and England and trading all the way. Then there's farming; an industry in which the Welsh have had to be in a state of almost permanent enterprise, to offset its relentless long-term decline. When you see the many and varied ways in which modern Welsh farmers have diversified, from specialist foods to moto-cross tracks, rare breed development to tourism, to new technology, you cannot possibly say that this is a race lacking in entrepreneurship.

Beyond the safe areas, where even the most recalcitrant Englishman may grudgingly agree that the Welsh have succeeded (agriculture, retail, literature and song, or as teachers and preachers), history is peppered with copious examples of Welsh success in science, engineering, transport and trade. But still the English assumption that the Welsh are economically useless, or that England subsidises Wales, lingers on. Barely a day goes by without a letter like this one appearing in a Welsh newspaper:

SIR – What a pity that Blair did not ask the English members of the United Kingdom whether there was a need for Welsh and Scottish Parliaments, especially as the English seem to be bearing the cost of these extravagant 'Europe-aligned' ventures.

When south-east England becomes a region of Europe, will they pump some water and gas under the Channel to meet current needs?

David Morgan of Solihull, the *Western Mail*, March 2006

Look on any internet site dealing with such matters, and you will find hundreds of contributors, saying much the same sort of thing, usually in far more expletive-laden ways. The central thrust is always the same: that Wales (and Scotland) get way more than their fair share of money and power, and that the poor taxpayers of England are forever giving hand-outs to the other parts of the UK. Some more rabid commentators take their thoughts further and regularly describe Wales as the 'Albania of the British Isles' (or of Western Europe), and declare that the Welsh economy would collapse without the munificence of the English tax-payer.

The figures show that the Wales-to-UK proportion in population, public expenditure and tax revenue are all fairly close, and that Wales, despite being one of the hardest-hit areas in western Europe, receives considerably less per capita than Scotland, Northern Ireland, or parts of England. In a way, however, that's not the point. Although the foaming-at-the-mouth English nationalists, who stalk the internet and are for ever ranting on radio phone-ins, would like to believe the same old rubbish (that Wales is an inherently unenterprising, needy place) that has been spouted for most of the last two hundred years, it is patently untrue. Even in the current situation, in the aftermath of the swingeing destruction of Welsh heavy industry and with an economy that is relegated to the status of marginal (see the chapter On the Edge), there is much potential in Wales. It exports gas, oil and refined oil, electricity, food and many industrial components. There are thriving information technology, specialist research and cultural industries. Perhaps most importantly, every pundit is pointing to water becoming the essential commodity of the next few decades; something that Wales has been exporting in huge quantity for over a century now (interestingly, English consumers generally pay considerably less for Welsh water than do customers in Wales). Many valuable minerals still lie within the Welsh landscape. Wales has all the ingredients for a successful, integrated economy, and all the necessary enterprise to make it happen.

'More culture in a Pot of Yoghurt'

Sex, money and religion are all areas of life that are predictable enough for a bit of Welsh-bashing, but it hasn't stopped there. Over the centuries, English writers and critics have made great play in trying to put Wales down as a cultural black hole, somewhere that has no creativity of note to boast about. This is an astonishing re-interpretation of the facts.

In his novel, *Decline and Fall* (1928), Evelyn Waugh stated it thus:

> *'The Welsh,' said the doctor, 'are the only nation in the world that has produced no graphic or plastic art, no architecture, no drama. They just sing,' he said with disgust, 'sing and blow down wind instruments of plated silver.'*

The novel is partly set in a thunderously shambolic private school in Wales, where the local silver band are invited to perform at sports day. To a man, they are all thick, low-browed and ape-like; they 'loped like wolves', while slavering over anything pretty in a skirt.

Contemporary novelist, critic and notable snob for all things English, A N Wilson (the Welsh are 'dingy, untalented and sly'), has made a number of similar points, including the quite breathtaking:

> *The Welsh have never made any significant contribution to any branch of knowledge, culture or entertainment. They have no architecture, no gastronomic tradition, no literature worthy of the name.*

This latter point, about a perceived lack of literature, is startling in its audacity, for literature in Welsh far pre-dates anything in English and, at every turn, has produced world-class poets and authors, who are often taken far more seriously outside of the UK than within it. Furthermore, Welsh culture – even today, in our supremely dumbed-down age – holds its writers and artists firmly centre stage in the national action, something you would be very hard pressed indeed to say about England.

As a case in point, and to finish this chapter where it began, here is the best answer possible to the mean-spirited Taffy is a Welshman nursery rhyme. You can rant, you can rave, or you can subvert it and turn it around into something of strength, beauty and power, as poet Alun Rees did – in characteristically Welsh style – in his superb anthology, *Yesterday's Tomorrow* (Y Lolfa, 2005):

TAFFY IS A WELSHMAN

Taffy is a Welshman,
Taffy is no thief.
Someone came to Taffy's house
and stole a leg of beef.

Taffy made no protest,
for he doesn't like a row,
so the someone called on him again
and stole the bloody cow.

They stole his coal and iron,
they stole his pastures, too.
They even stole his language
and flushed it down the loo.

Taffy is a Welshman,
Taffy is a fool.
Taffy voted no, no, no
when they offered him home rule.

Six days a week upon his knees
Taffy dug for coal.
On the seventh he was kneeling, too,
praying for his soul.

And now the mines are closing down
and chapel's had its day,
Taffy still lives upon his knees,
for he knows no other way.

Now sometimes Taffy's brother
will start a row or so,
but you can bank on Taffy:
he doesn't want to know.

For when they hanged Penderyn
he had nothing much to say,
and when Saunders Lewis went to jail
he looked the other way.

Taffy is a Welshman
who likes to be oppressed.
He was proud to tug his forelock
to a Crawshay or a Guest.

They give him tinsel royals,
so he has a pint of beer,
and sings God Bless the Prince of Wales
as he joins the mob to cheer.

Now Taffy is a fighter
when he hears the bugle call.
Name any war since Agincourt:
Taffy's seen them all.

He's fought in France and Germany
and many another land;
he's fought by sea and fought by air
and fought on desert sand.

He's fought for many a foreign flag
in many a foreign part,
for Taffy is a Welshman,
proud of his fighting heart.

He's fought the wide world over,
he's given blood and bone.
He's fought for every bloody cause
except his bloody own.

Chapter 2

CRAKING AND BABBLING:
The Welsh Language

The people of the dominion [Wales] have and do daily use a speech nothing like nor consonant to the natural mother tongue used within this realm... No person or persons that use the Welsh speech or language shall have or enjoy any manor, office or fees within the realm of England, Wales or other the king's dominions upon pain of forfeiting the same offices or fees unless he or they use and exercise the speech or language of English.

The Act of Union between England and Wales, 1536

More than any other aspect of Wales and Welshness, it is *Cymraeg*, the Welsh language, that provides by far the biggest lightning conductor for antipathy between the neighbouring nations. When the BBC, in the early 1990s, experimented with showing the Welsh language soap, *Pobol y Cwm*, across the whole of Britain on daytime BBC2 (with subtitles), their switchboards nearly blew up. 'Get that language of the devil off our screens,' caller after caller from suburban Middle England demanded, much to the surprise of the schedulers, who had – hitherto correctly – assumed that they could put any old cobblers on in the afternoon and the audience would either be too brain-dead, too stoned or too bored to complain. A zillion makeover shows and life-threatening overdoses of Ainsley Harriott passed by unremarked. But drop in a little slice of Cwmderi life, and all hell broke loose. The deepest of raw nerves had evidently been resoundingly struck.

It is incontrovertibly true that *Cymraeg* succeeds in both

terrifying and offending many English people. Faces go crimson, breath gets that little bit shorter and pulse-rates quicken at the sight or sound of this particular grouping of vowels and consonants. How on earth could a mere language be credited with such power? For deep and startling power it certainly has, and this particular power has been around for a very long time.

Part of the explanation, for sure, is that English people are generally suspicious of any language other than their own. So used are they to the world's affairs being conducted in their own tongue, that any other, be it French, Spanish, Cantonese, Welsh or Swahili, is viewed with, at best, a kind of patronising sympathy and, at worst, downright hostility. The popular image of the Englishman abroad, talking ever louder in English until the exasperated locals pretend to understand, is no work of fiction. But such stubborn monolingualism is not just reserved for those on their IntaSun fortnight. Go to any of the Costas or the Canary Islands and you'll meet leathery old English ex-pats, who've lived there for ten years and who, between jugs of sangria, boast loudly that they've never bothered learning more than two words of Spanish. To them, it's a badge of pride.

How much more acute the situation is, therefore, in *y Fro Gymraeg*, Welsh-speaking Wales. At least the orange-skinned alcoholics in Gran Canaria don't take offence if they hear Pedro and Ramon conversing in Spanish. They are usually just about gracious enough to realise that it is, after all, their country and their language. But if they overhear two Welsh speakers in Dolgellau, comparable feelings of charity don't even make it out of the starting blocks. Something deep inside them stirs, and they feel slighted, insulted, excluded. Welsh speakers are only using the language 'to prove a point'. They only ever speak Welsh when English people are around to hear

www.Cartoonstock.com

them. Even 'unpronounceable' Welsh place names, hundreds, sometimes even thousands, of years old, 'are put there simply as an elaborate joke.' (Peter Paterson in the *Daily Mail*). As self-flattery and self-absorption go, it's pretty hard to beat.

It is, I believe, almost impossible to overstate this. People are really, truly offended by folk using their own language in their own country. I have witnessed it on numerous occasions, when Welsh is greeted by a flash of pure anger in the eyes, which then, thanks to the niceties of social training, quickly mellows out into a sort of low-level paranoia. Its success in being much, much more of an irritant to many English people than any other language is, I believe, thanks to a mysterious, lurking, collective memory that hangs in our island ether. As *Lord of the Rings* author, J R R Tolkien, put it, 'Welsh is of this soil, this island, the senior language of the men of Britain; and Welsh is beautiful.' This incontrovertible truth is at the root of the hostility, a lurking terror that there is something older and more settled about their land that English people do not have access to. As a result, much of the terminology used over the centuries about Welsh has been deliberately apocalyptic, for it is seen in terms of a fierce battle; one that English must be seen to win, to be the vanquishing hero. The battle has been conducted on a number of fronts over the centuries, but they all fall within a predictable few areas and these never seem to change.

It is often said that Welsh people themselves have been their own worst enemy with regards to the language. Even now, many south Walians of a certain age note with great regret how their Cymraeg-speaking parents and grandparents denied them their native tongue, a very widespread process that has left many Welsh people cut loose from their own culture. But even this awful, disempowering process was a product of English condescension and strident anti-Welsh sentiment. So thoroughly were Wales and Welsh belittled and discouraged, small wonder that thousands of Welsh people were led inevitably to the conclusion that the only way they could achieve any sort of parity with their 'superior' neighbours was by ditching their native language and embracing English. The option of using both languages fluently and happily, side-by-side, was never really countenanced until comparatively recently, by which time it was too late for many.

Many of the brickbats that have been hurled towards the Welsh language over the centuries fall into a small number of predictable, and seemingly eternal, categories.

'Welsh Is a Dead Language'

If you believed the obituaries, the Welsh language has had more comebacks than Tom Jones. It has been declared to be almost dead on a very regular basis, since the nineteenth century, and, until quite recently, this has invariably been presented as a desirable state of affairs. Even before Victorian times, though, when the vast majority of people in Wales were monoglot Welsh speakers, many English visitors found the language deeply disturbing, and wished it dead:

> *Their native gibberish is usually prattled throughout the whole of Taphydom except in their market towns, whose inhabitants, being a little raised, do begin to despise it. If the stars prove lucky, there may be some glimmering hopes that the British language may be quite extinct and may be English'd out of Wales.*

William Richards, Wallography, 1682

Over three centuries later, Welsh stubbornly continues to refuse to be English'd out, but that doesn't stop the jibes of those who would like to have us believe that this growing language, spoken by over half a million people in Wales, and perhaps as many again elsewhere, lies a-moulderin' in its grave. Our old friend A A Gill in his *Sunday Times* TV column, for example:

> *Just to prove there is at least the echo of life from the pit of extinction, BBC2 last Sunday gave us the bardic version of Jurassic Park: Ku Klux Druids. The National Eisteddfod of Wales. Ha-ha-ha-ha-ha. Or as they say in Wales: Llha-llha.*

If the language can be written off so peremptorily, then that, of course, lets those with any kind of responsibility for aiding it off the hook. Government ministers, for example, such as the late George Brown, who, as the Labour Party's Secretary of State for the Department of Economic Affairs, boomed in a speech at Bangor in 1965: 'The price of a pound of beef is more important than your bloody language.' Perhaps he confused a pound of beef with a bottle of vodka. A legion of Labour politicians, Welsh as well as English, have demonstrated similar haughty dismissal of the language, none more notable or vocal than Neil Kinnock, whose anti-devolution campaign of 1979 almost entirely revolved around spreading the scare in south Wales that a Welsh Assembly would mean domination by a 'Welsh-speaking elite'. His paranoia about the language is perhaps the only consistent political stance he has managed, particularly since this one-time anti-EU, anti-House of Lords firebrand entered the Lords as Baron Kinnock of Bedwellty, having just given up his post as an EU commissioner (on a lovely fat pension). Glenys, his wife and now one of Wales' Members of the European Parliament, is a Welsh-speaker from Anglesey, but the Kinnocks, despite their latter conversion to a multi-lingual Europe, didn't bother to pass the language on to their own children.

Remarkably, commentators have managed over the years simultaneously to condemn the Welsh language as dead, dying or useless, while marvelling at its widespread usage. One telling entry in a School Inspector's log book of 1878 came from his visit to the school at Llanrug, near Caernarfon. 'Few of them show intelligence. I find that when the question is translated to Welsh, they understand it better.' You don't say.

Even when the Welsh language resolutely proves to English eyes and ears that it is far from dead, few London critics believe it. The lovely film, *Hedd Wyn*, was nominated for the best foreign language film Oscar in 1994, a turn of events that brought nothing but snooty put-downs from the film critics in England, none more so than in the liberal press. *The Guardian* reported that 'even the Welsh' were going to the Oscars, thanks to this 'little-known and even less-seen film.' (Eh? No distributors for

English cinemas would touch a Welsh language movie, and England's Channel 4 only decided hastily to screen *Hedd Wyn* once it had garnered its Oscar nomination, a situation that would never arise for any other major movie produced from within the UK). Sometimes, it takes recognition from beyond this little island to remind the English that Welsh is neither dead nor dying, and that it punches its weight with great aplomb in the cultural sphere. And when they are reminded, they really don't like it very much.

'Welsh Is an Ugly Language'

This is one of the commonest aspersions aimed at *Cymraeg*. It's been repeated so often, it's almost a given fact to the English. And this is from the tongue that has given us such mellifluous words as gobble, acne, Grimsby and wanker. Poetry indeed.

Underpinning most of the snide asides about the perceived ugliness of the Welsh tongue is a much-repeated maxim, that the language sounds archaic, depending on guttural sounds and phlegmatic noises rather than the sweet, sophisticated flow of a renaissance language such as modern English. Like so many other aspects of Welsh life, the language is deemed to be a relic blasted directly from an uncivilised age, when grunts and coarse noises passed for communication. Mention the Welsh language to most English people and you can guarantee that someone will crack the ancient joke that it is 'English without the vowels' (Jeremy Clarkson and very many others), or 'a bad Scrabble hand'. Even good leftie comedians, with right-on credentials as long as your arm, can't resist the old clichés. Mark Steel, the long-standing Socialist Workers' Party member, launched a tired old lob at the language on the BBC comedy show *QI*, wondering why the words-and-numbers quiz game, *Countdown*, was shown on S4C, the Welsh Channel 4. In a mock Welsh accent, he droned, 'I'll have a consonant, please, Carol. And another one. Another twenty-seven consonants, please. And a consonant.' It might be news to him, and the many others who have made the same side-splitting joke, but there are actually seven vowels in Welsh (a, e, i, o, u, w, y), as against five in English. Never let the facts get in the way of the punch line, though.

A popular comparison has been between the words of *Cymraeg* and the noises of animals. An English nobleman's account of his 1700 trip to North Wales declaimed that, 'The language is inarticulate and guttural and sounds more like the gobbling of geese or turkeys than the speech of rational creatures.' The eighteenth century was a time when many well-

The arrival of some Welsh programming on the BBC led to the inevitable sneers from the London press, such as this example by Joseph Lee from the *Evening News* of June 1935. The caption reads: *'No, there's nothing wrong with the car, dear. It's just that Welsh programme on the wireless.'*

By permission of Associated Newspapers/Solo Syndication and thanks to the Centre for the Study of Cartoons and Caricature, University of Kent at Canterbury to-do English folk trotted around Wales, often keeping journals that scoffed heartily at the language. One John Torbuck, in his 1749 memoir of a *grand tour* through Wales, noted, "tis a tongue (it seems) not made for any mouth; as appears by an instance of one in our company who, having got a Welsh polysyllable into his throat, was almost choked with consonants, had we not, by clapping him on the back, made him disgorge a guttural or two, and so saved him.' It's the joke that refuses to die, and keeps re-appearing down the centuries. Perennial sniper, A A Gill, in *The Sunday Times*, called Welsh 'the tongue of the glottally challenged,' while a 2005 property puff in the *Telegraph*, for a Welsh farmhouse, said that the property's name, 'Like so much in Welsh, sounds like a murderous threat uttered by a man preparing to spit.'

More modern commentators have taken this further by using the language to portray Welsh speakers as little more than spitting buffoons. 'If you ask for directions in Wales, you'll have to wash the spit out of your hair,' cracked Blackadder (Rowan Atkinson), in the eponymous BBC comedy series, echoing Evelyn Waugh, who had written, 'Everyone in Wales has black spittle and whenever he meets you, he says *borra-da* and spits.' Edwardian postcards harped on much the same point, choosing only to mock the supposedly unpronounceable Welsh place names, while steadfastly ignoring the fact that, once the few basic rules are learnt, place names – and, indeed, all other words in Welsh – become supremely pronounceable, for they are almost universally regular. This, it should be remembered, is in sharp contrast to English place names, which show a bewildering irregularity in their pronunciation, as anyone who has sought directions to Leominster, Loughborough, Greenwich, Alnwick, Caldmore, Thame and Southwark would wearily testify.

It's a simple equation. English is rational, reasonable, smooth and urbane. It *sounds* contemporary, flowing freely like a gentle breeze. By contrast, Welsh is animalistic, jerky, spit-laden and harsh as an old sack, a series of oral gusts and gales that blow the unsuspecting listeners off their comfortable perches. And there are certainly truths here: to speak Welsh demands a different set of sounds and facial movements, especially for the English-speaking mouth. All learners spend their early months grappling with the *ll*, *ngh* and *ch* sounds in particular, demanding, as they do, a completely new arrangement of teeth and tongue. Such sounds *feel* more ancient, as if they have been drawn from a deeper, darker well of the human vocal range.

Observations about the comparative sounds of the English and Welsh languages are often bizarre enough. But when they are extrapolated further, into assumptions about what the difference in sound means in terms of either language's level of sophistication, breadth of scope, or sheer raw power, then things get very strange indeed. It's one thing to sneer at Welsh as inarticulate and guttural, but another entirely therefore to decide, with no actual knowledge of the language, that it is incapable of sustaining itself in a modern setting. It's back to the animal noises all over again – just as we assume that dogs or donkeys cannot converse in the same way that we can, so do many people assume that the Welsh language cannot express the same breadth of experience as more renaissance tongues, most notably English.

'The Secret Language of Extremists'

'The continuance of the language is... kept up... to keep the dissenters together,' wrote E P Richards, in a letter to the Marquis of Bute, in 1833. While there is inevitably a certain thrill of exclusivity to be had from communicating in a language inaccessible to others around, this is possibly the strangest misunderstanding about the Welsh language, that it is only ever used as a 'secret' tongue, like the Twilight Bark in *101 Dalmations,* or some wartime code beep-beeping its way to foreign fields from Bletchley Park. This paranoia fuels all of the old assumptions that the language is therefore used only by political extremists, as a way of passing on information unavailable to 'moderate' (i.e. non-Welsh speaking) people.

This became glaringly obvious to me as soon as I started to learn Welsh. In that fit of zeal that nearly always accompanies any new undertaking in life, I decided to put a Welsh, as well as English, message on my telephone answering machine. But because my Welsh was, at best, sketchy, the Welsh part of the message contained an extra sentence. *'Os dych chi'n gadael neges yn Gymraeg, siaradwch yn araf i-a-w-n, os gwelwch yn dda'* (If you're leaving a message in Welsh, please speak v-e-r-y slowly.) This made the Welsh section of the message (which was first) quite a bit longer than the English section that followed.

Immediately, the suspicious voices of friends and relatives would greet me on my return home. 'You say a lot more in Welsh,' just about every other caller would say, before pausing. 'Are you giving out some sort of secret message just for Welsh speakers?' as if my telephone answering machine was exhorting people to bomb the nearest holiday home as well as confirm that they could meet me later for a pint. It was Welsh. It was a bit longer. Therefore, it could only be a conspiracy. Wow!

When it comes to English incomers and their relationship with the language, part of the problem is that their experience of Wales has, up to the point of moving, largely been as tourists in the country. Exposure to Cymraeg is sketchy at best for tourists. For starters, they are more likely to be staying, eating and drinking in places surrounded by other visitors, mostly monoglot English speakers. Then you have to remember (as is explored further in the chapter entitled The Good Life) that the majority of the Welsh tourist industry is run by English people, many of whom give the Welsh language only token recognition, if at all. How different it is when they move here, suddenly finding themselves in communities where the language is the staple of everyday life. It's a shock from which some never recover, and it only fuels the feelings of exclusion from a 'secret' life going on around them.

The idea that the Welsh language is the sole preserve of extremists is very well rooted. In the early days of the BBC, during the 1930s, the Wales and the West regional supremo, Bristol-based E R Appleton, responded thus to a letter from Saunders Lewis, who had requested there might be some programmes in Welsh, and that Wales be granted regional status of its own:

Wales, of its own choice, is a part of the British Commonwealth of Nations, whose official language is English. When His Majesty's Government decided to establish a Corporation for the important task of broadcasting it was natural that the official language alone should be used... To use the ancient languages regularly – Welsh, Irish, Gaelic and Manx – would be either to serve propaganda purposes or to disregard the needs of the greatest number in the interests of those who use the languages for aesthetic and sentimental reasons rather than for practical purposes... If the extremists, who want to force the Welsh language on the listeners of the region, should get their way, the official language would lose its grip.

Step back from the argument, and this is an astonishing train of thought. Just how extreme or propagandist can talking to people in their first language be? If it is the language in which they chat and gossip with their neighbours, do their shopping, express their affection and disdain alike, what earthly reason can there be for not allowing them to be broadcast to in that same language? Consider, too, that at this time there were still considerable numbers of people in Wales who, for all practical purposes, spoke no other language at all. They were not trying to prove a point, be subversive or undermine the status quo. They were merely communicating in the language of their community, in the only way that they knew how. And that was enough for them to be seen by officialdom as self-declared extremists.

Part of this bizarre generalisation is the unshakeable belief that Welsh speakers only use the language to exclude monoglot English speakers. Thus, the assumption runs, they only switch to Welsh when an English speaker is within earshot. We've all heard the countless stories of the 'I went into a shop and they all changed to Welsh' variety, presumably from people with such sharp hearing that they can tell precisely what language folk are chatting in, way before they've even entered the room.

This weary cliché is trotted out so often that it has become one of the staples of Welsh comedy. Take this contribution, for example, from a book published in 1994:

> *If an Englishman enters a shop in Welsh-speaking parts of Wales, the locals are likely to switch promptly to speaking Welsh. Thus the Englishman cannot be sure whether they are talking about him.*

Who was the author of this corny old guff? Some harrumphing old buffer recently retired to Prestatyn? Why, no, it was none other than the man who, at the time it was written, was occupying the post of Secretary of State for Wales in Her Majesty's Government. John Redwood – for it is he – was perhaps the ultimate Tory Welsh Secretary. When Margaret Thatcher was first elected, in 1979, she made at least the token effort of installing MPs who represented Welsh constituencies into the office of Secretary of State for what Tories always love to call The Principality, as if Wales was some mock-feudal Liechtenstein or Monaco. This all changed in 1987, when incumbent Nicholas Edwards left the House of Commons at that year's general election. Thatcher was eager to sideline the moderate Peter Walker, MP for Worcester, and in Tory eyes, the job of Welsh Secretary is only marginally higher up the rankings than that of the person who brings round the biscuits at Cabinet meetings. True to form for the bitter old bag, Walker was shunted into the job, and it was widely – and correctly – seen as a savage demotion.

Peter Walker was the first non-Welsh Secretary of State. The justification was that his seat of Worcester was, well, quite near the border. If you stood on top of the tower of Worcester Cathedral, you could probably even see the distant blue humps of Wales on the horizon. Perfect. And thus a trend was set. When Thatcher finally plucked up the courage to do what she'd always wanted to do anyway – namely, sack Peter Walker outright – she placed David Hunt, MP for the Wirral constituency of Birkenhead (a place so near Wales it had even hosted the National Eisteddfod once), in the job. Then, Thatcher herself was unceremoniously dumped by her party, and mild-mannered John Major, the boy who ran away from a circus to become an accountant, became Prime Minister.

David Hunt was a favourite of Major, so his days languishing in the Tory dungeon of the Welsh Office were obviously numbered. And so it transpired; in 1993, he was promoted to Secretary of State for Employment, and Major looked around his parliamentary party for a replacement to send to Cardiff. Having seen the link between Wales and the job of Secretary of State gingerly broken by Margaret Thatcher, Major snapped it completely and appointed the arch-monetarist John Redwood, a man with all the human warmth of rickets, to the job. Even the most loyal Tory couldn't stretch the geography of the country and pretend that Redwood's constituency of Wokingham, in Surrey, was anywhere near the Severn Bridge. Reactions in Wales varied between utter incredulity and stunned outrage. The man knew nothing about Wales, cared even less, refused to spend a night here and swiftly set on a course of offending as many Welsh people as possible. His party was rewarded at the next general election with a complete wipe-out west of Offa's Dyke.

And thus it was that the Secretary of State for Wales came to put his suburban English prejudices about his new fiefdom into print. He was also famous for refusing to sign any Welsh Office documents printed in Cymraeg, lest some sneaky civil servant was getting him to sign an execution order on all English people, or a decree that all Welsh Office mandarins should be rewarded with an instant 100% pay rise. However, with the benefit of hindsight, we can surely forgive him, because he left us with one of the greatest moments of pure, pant-wetting comedy that has ever graced British TV screens. At a Welsh Tory conference, the blue rinses broke into a wheezy rendition of *Hen Wlad Fy Nhadau*, and Redwood, despite knowing not one word of the national anthem, thought no-one would notice if he just pretended to sing along. To the eternal gratitude of us all, a TV cameraman kept his camera trained on Redwood throughout, thus catching him opening and shutting his mouth like a startled goldfish, and bobbing his head from side to side in a lamentable attempt to demonstrate a sense of rhythm. That TV clip was voted one of the best of all time, in a UK-wide poll at the end of 1999. It is perfection. S4C should show it every night at 6pm, just like RTE do in Ireland with the Angelus, the Catholic call to prayer. Nothing would unite the nation more.

Despite the new-look Tories we see today (saved from

extinction in Wales, it should be remembered, by the arrival of the National Assembly, a body they spat bile at from the word go), the Conservative party in London has never much understood or cared for Wales. In 1972, Lord Hailsham (né Quintin Hogg), the Lord Chancellor, addressed the Welsh Conservative conference. It was a time when Welsh politics was hotting up a little, with flashpoints such as reservoirs, campaigns for bilingual signs, the Prince of Wales' investiture, and soaring support for Plaid Cymru. In his speech, Hailsham showed the depths of government paranoia in his hyperbole about *Cymdeithas yr Iaith*, the Welsh Language Society: 'The thing which differentiates them [*Cymdeithas*] from the baboons of the IRA, who blow the arms and legs off innocent women and children, and break the knees and tar the bodies of pregnant women, and shoot our lads in the streets of Londonderry and Belfast, is basically a question of degree and not kind.' To see such a parallel, between paramilitary terrorists blowing up pubs and an organisation whose most revolutionary act was daubing road signs, was particularly revealing, and showed a monumental lack of both perspective and understanding of the problem.

Too many propagandists have attempted to make the usage of, or support for, the Welsh language, in any form, automatically equate with extremism. In modern times, perhaps the worst culprit was Paul Starling, the political editor of the short-lived Welsh edition of the *Daily Mirror*, which came into existence in 1999 with the advent of the National Assembly, but which was closed down by its parent company in the summer of 2003. The first Assembly elections in 1999 saw the Labour party's support slump, largely in favour of Plaid Cymru, who even captured seats such as Rhondda and Islwyn, in the Valleys where, traditionally, Labour majorities had been in the tens of thousands. The *Welsh*

Mirror was strictly, stridently loyal to its Labour masters: almost alone, it supported the ailing First Minister, Alun Michael, in the Assembly's first big scrap (Michael resigned nonetheless), but its major legacy was a constant drip-drip diet of anti-Plaid Cymru and anti-Welsh language scare stories, all written by Paul Starling. It worked: in the second round of Assembly elections, in May 2003, Plaid's support plummeted and they lost their Valleys seats. Shortly afterwards, the plug was pulled on the *Welsh Mirror*, its job well done.

There are so many examples of Starling's vitriolic hysteria and his constant conflation of support for the Welsh language with political extremism (see the archive on Labour MP Paul Flynn's website: www.paulflynnmp.co.uk for some of the most hair-raising specimens), but I'll content myself here with what seemed to me the worst. In the run-up to the 2002 National Eisteddfod in Pembrokeshire, Starling went into overdrive to smear the festival, its place in Welsh society (and beyond; this is, after all, Europe's largest indigenous cultural knees-up) and, by extrapolation, all who attended. It kicked off with a headline on the Friday prior to the week of the Eisteddfod: TIME FOR THE FESTIVAL OF FEAR AND HATRED it screamed, over apocalyptic warnings by Paul Starling that, the Eisteddfod will be the trigger for violence, and that people were living in fear of language extremists. Needless to say, the most terrifying thing that happened that week was an abundance of torrential rain and some badly-cooked burgers, but the damage had surely already been done.

This all said, there are, of course, a few nuggets of truth amidst the anti-Cymraeg paranoia. There *is* a delicious feeling in being able to conduct a private, secret conversation, when people around do not understand the language that you're using, and, naturally enough, many Welsh speakers (or speakers of any other minority language) will do that on occasion. But the subversive nature of such an action has been created by centuries of anti-Welsh officialdom and attitude. It has become a self-fulfilling prophecy. Until only very, very recently, Welsh had had almost no legal or official status since the Middle Ages; since then, it has been seen as renegade and rebellious, a vernacular barely to be tolerated, let alone encouraged. Small wonder that the taint of rebellion has seeped into its usage; it has been forcibly done by those who wish it ill. As author Gwyn Thomas wrote in his journal in 1970, 'The Welsh language has become in both senses a club: it is a conspiracy of people seeking preferment through the speaking of an arcane tongue; it is an offensive weapon for use against the British government.' In an age when dumbed-down, mass marketing techniques, often culled from expert understanding of how to brainwash or hypnotise people, are used as an excuse for our governance, long may Welsh continue to be a much-needed offensive weapon.

'Not a Civilised Language'

The belief that Welsh is used only for extreme, or political, or secretive means has, over the centuries, been broadened out into its (il)logical conclusion; namely, that the language is a huge drawback to the civilisation of Wales. And by civilisation, commentators generally mean a very specific type: Anglicisation. Underpinning all the comments is the unshakeable English certainty that their breed of good manners and gentility, combined with a tendency towards colonialism, is the only one that counts. To the English, their language is the fundamental core of such values; even if they rather conveniently forget that it is only the world's *lingua franca* thanks to the superpower status of the USA.

An editorial in *The Times* from September 1866 puts the case most forcibly. 'The Welsh language is the curse of Wales. Its prevalence and the ignorance of English have excluded, and even now exclude, the Welsh people from the civilization, the improvement, and the material prosperity of their English neighbours... Their antiquated and semi-barbarous language, in short, shrouds them in darkness.' Just a week later, The Thunderer continued with a further editorial rant, inspired by the National Eisteddfod. 'The Eisteddfod is one of the most mischievous and selfish pieces of sentimentalism which could possibly be perpetrated. It is simply a foolish interference with the natural progress of civilization and prosperity. If it is desirable that the Welsh should talk English, it is monstrous folly to encourage them in a loving fondness for their old language.'

This 'loving fondness for their old language' was, in truth, something much simpler. Huge numbers of people spoke only Welsh at this time; there was nothing soppy or sentimental about their use of the language; it was as natural to their lives and communities as fresh air or water. We cannot be absolutely sure of numbers of Welsh speakers at this time, as the first census to include language did not occur until 1891. That showed some 54.4 per cent of the Welsh population (910,000 people) spoke Welsh, over half a million of them with no English at all. Thirty years earlier, the proportion and number of monoglot Welsh speakers would have been far higher, and it was against this sort of backdrop that such pompous pronouncements were being made in London.

This period of the mid nineteenth century saw the harshest, and most consistent, attacks on Cymraeg from official quarters. The Education Commissioners' Report of 1847 (a.k.a. the Blue Books – see the chapter The Welsh Character for more on this) was utterly unambiguous in its conclusion that, 'The Welsh language is a vast drawback to Wales, and a manifold barrier to the moral progress and commercial prosperity of the people. It is not easy to over-estimate its evil effects.' The *moral* progress? There it is again – speak the language of the animals, and you'll end up behaving like one. Strangely, it was the Victorian explosion of chapel-building, those most morally erect of institutions, that was largely responsible for the widespread promulgation of the Welsh language, but you'd never know it from these sweeping condemnations aimed at it. And it wasn't just the English having a pop: the Anglo-Welsh gentry weighed in with similarly totalitarian warnings, such as this, given in a speech by Henry Bruce, later the first Baron Aberdare, in 1851: 'I consider the Welsh language a serious evil, a great obstruction to the moral and intellectual progress of my countrymen.' Aberdare was a self-declared expert in 'civilisation'; it was under his governorship that the National African Company bullied and bribed its way into colonising what is now Nigeria, in the latter part of the nineteenth century.

'Not a Proper Language'

Then there are the doubts deep down in many monoglot English speakers that, just as Wales itself is not a 'proper' country, neither is Welsh a 'proper' language. People who have no knowledge of the tongue, save for *Teleffon* and *Toiledau*, proclaim with absolute certainty that Welsh speakers cannot understand each other beyond their own *milltir sgwar*, because, of course, the Welsh language is little more than a guttural series of grunts, in almost entirely different dialects. One Englishman in Ceredigion gleefully told me the story of how the new National Assembly had ground to a halt, in its early days, because people from Sir Fôn couldn't understand the folk from Sir Benfro. This picture of a latter-day Tower of Babel, with a few dozen Welsh men and women jabbering uselessly at each other, in dialects incomprehensible to anyone else, may well give comfort to the anti-Cymraeg brigade, but it is, I'm sorry to have to tell them, utter bollocks. And neither is it a view reserved just for *Sun*-reading boneheads; one correspondent in that Bible of liberal England, *The Guardian*, wrote, after the devolution referendum, that he hoped that its success would mean, 'That it will be made illegal to speak the unintelligent gibberish called Welsh outside Wales.'

This suspicion most readily rears its head in English minds when they hear a Welsh sentence being spoken which contains any non-Welsh (usually, not surprisingly given the realities of geography and history, English) words within it. We've all heard the pub comedians with their lame impersonations of Welsh sentences ('Achy yachy dachy *ambulance* yachy yachy llareggub achy *microwave oven*,' and so on). Proof, they crow, that Welsh is not a proper language. Even quite well-meaning people often pick up on this point, as if the inevitable mingling of English words with Welsh is somehow confirmation that the language is unable to cope with either complexity, subtlety, or the modern world. As Glenda Jackson, actress-turned-Labour MP, put it on HTV's *Art & Soul* programme, in 1989, 'I have doubts about Welsh being a language that is sufficiently expressive for cultural purposes.' No, the language that has sparkled for around two millennia, through the medium of some of the world's most exquisitely precise poetry and song, couldn't possibly be 'sufficiently expressive for cultural purposes'.

In the same vein, Janet Street-Porter, that nemesis of Welsh language culture, was characteristically blunt in the *Independent on Sunday* in 2001: 'When you consider that the

"I haven't the foggiest idea. What does yours say?"

Beneath the reasonable brow of many an English bigot beats a brain quietly convinced that Welsh isn't a real language or that people are making it up as they go along, as this June 1969 example by Keith Waite from the *Sun* amply demonstrates.

By permission of Keith Waite and the *Sun*; thanks to the Centre for the Study of Cartoons and Caricature, University of Kent at Canterbury

Welsh language is only kept alive by committees inventing new words for modern inventions like the motor car and the television set, you don't know whether to laugh or cry.' The best answer to that comes from 1907, rather showing that Janet's tendentious tirade is nothing new. In a book entitled *Wales*

Today and Tomorrow, Edward Anwyl wrote: 'The mistake often made by many people outside Wales who think of the Welsh language is that of supposing that it has no natural spontaneous life and that it is kept alive merely by a process of artificial respiration.'

Do these people go into similar fits of sniggering or haughty condescension when they hear English people talking about their *raison d'être*, the fact that they live in a *cul-de-sac*, or felt a shiver of *déja-vu*, or the delicious tang of *Schadenfreude*? Like all languages, English is a hybrid of every other tongue and has taken words in their thousands from French, German, Greek and Latin. Very many of our most common words were nicked from other languages, such as Spanish (playing *guitar* with an *alligator* in a *hurricane* is a *breeze*, compared with smoking *tobacco* and *marijuana*, or eating *banana* and *chocolate* in a *cafeteria*); Arabic (the *admiral*, reading a *magazine* about *alcohol*, applied his *mascara* on the *cotton sofa*). And what of the Welsh contributions to the English language (*Dad!* The *corgi*'s had a *wee* on the *penguin* in the *crockery booth*!)? All languages are organic beasts that adapt with time, magpies that cherry-pick what they want or need from other tongues; to be so selective about one language's usage within another (as seems almost exclusively to happen with English words in Welsh) is just plain snippy, and rather tellingly loaded.

Another facet of the belief that Welsh is not a proper language comes about because there are no real monoglot Welsh speakers left. Everyone of school age and above in Wales can, in this day and age, manage some English, and that fact sits brooding deeply in many English hearts as proof positive that Welsh is only used for somehow improper, or subversive means. It's a school of thought that goes back a long way and can be heard seeping through the lines of English poet Robert Graves' 1929 poem, *Welsh Incident*:

> *The populations of Pwllheli, Criccieth,*
> *Portmadoc, Borth, Tremadoc, Penrhyndeudraeth,*
> *Were all assembled. Criccieth's mayor addressed them*
> *First in good Welsh and then in fluent English...*

I *can* speak some French, but it doesn't mean that I want to all the time, or that I can express myself well enough in it for all occasions, and so it is with English, for many first-language Welsh speakers. And just because English seems so all-pervasive via television and technology, don't assume that everyone is at the same level. I've met many older people in areas like the Llŷn peninsula and Meirionydd who really don't have a great deal of English at their command, who use it sparingly, stiltingly and very rarely indeed. Even amongst younger people, there are many who are a fraction as comfortable and confident in English as they are in Welsh.

> *I will never be one of the natives, but my sons are Waunfawr boys. Children here are village property, known and loved by all. I see my sons growing up stable and confident, accepted for what they are by the close-knit village community. Moreover, I see them growing up as Welsh speakers. Some people are shocked that their English is so sketchy, and consider them deprived. But they are privileged. Their English will improve, but Welsh will be the language of their hearts, and they will have had a priceless gift, a bulwark against the flood of the monolithic, vapid Anglo-American culture which has swept through our country in recent decades.*
>
> Sylvia Prys Jones, *Discovering Welshness*

Or, as Ioan Bowen Rees put it, in a 1990 edition of the magazine *Planet: The Welsh Internationalist*: 'We bring up our children to speak Welsh not for the sake of the language, but for the sake of our children.'

This all said, perhaps some blame for misconceptions about the Welsh language should lie with those who most loudly proclaim the urgency of its survival. A common perception is that Welsh is languishing on its deathbed, a terminally ill patient, in dire need of regular transfusions of new laws, new money and new force-fed recruits. Although the language has taken a battering over the last century, it is too easy to over-state the case and create a permanent doom cloud over any consideration of Cymraeg. When all anyone ever hears about Welsh is that it is near its last gasp, you can hardly blame some people for failing to understand how deep-rooted, cherished and widespread it actually is. And it is.

'Forcing it Down our Throats'

History shows that, before a kind of liveable equilibrium is reached in practically any difficult area, the pendulum has to swing too far one way, then too far the other, before settling into a workable solution somewhere in the middle. This is highly pertinent when you examine official policy towards Welsh. Many people waste no time in moaning like stuck pigs that the Welsh language is forced on them, or that too much money is wasted on promoting it. If, however, with the benefit of a bit of historical perspective, we just compare these pro-Welsh policies, which have only been in place for twenty or so years, with the hundreds and hundreds of years of brutal, official suppression of the language, then it becomes abundantly clear that some sort of recent redressing of the balance (or, rather, imbalance) is not only hugely overdue and desirable, but is actually far less than it could, and perhaps should, be.

Not, of course, that this stops the scoffers. Every attempt to replace a monoglot English presence with at least a token bilingualism has been guaranteed to bring on the sneers and the wise-cracks. Even just spelling words and place names according to Welsh syntax, rather than English, causes haughty piss-taking, such as this from professional malevolent, Sir Kingsley Amis, in his 1986 novel, *The Old Devils*: 'They went outside and stood where a sign used to say Taxi and now said Taxi/Tacsi for the benefit of Welsh people who had never seen a letter x before.' And where would every local rag's letters page be without the occasional outburst from the usual nutters, telling the world that they are proud to live in Conway, not Conwy, or Caernarvon, rather than Caernarfon? Some folk in Ceredigion have even taken to blaming the county council's adoption of that ancient name, rather than the anglicized Cardiganshire that was in use until 1974, for a drop in tourist numbers to the area, as if legions of merry Midlanders set off for their jaunt to Aberporth, but got confused at the county border and turned back, muttering darkly to themselves.

Because place and house names are often some people's only contact with the Welsh language, it's not surprising that these have become a lightning conductor for the most determined of anti-Welsh bigots in our midst. There's even someone, up in Snowdonia, of all places, who runs a service to help people choose nice, new English names for their properties, when they swan in. Welsh names, that often are so beautifully descriptive and poetic, names that have survived hundreds of years in many cases, get unceremoniously chucked into the bin, and the houses are re-christened Mountain View, or named (as a property near me has been) after their egomaniac owners. And then there are those who live in a place for years, and who never even bother to learn how to pronounce their address properly. I was once on a TV programme, discussing English in-migration into Wales. One of the other contributors was an English malcontent who firmly believed that 'they force Welsh down your throat' (he actually used those words, the biggest cliché of all for anti-Welsh ranters. The now defunct Welsh edition of the *Daily Mirror*, which was vitriolic in its hatred of the language, even went so far as to publish a crass cartoon, showing someone having the word 'Welsh' literally, you know, forced down their throat. Subtle they weren't). The bloke on this TV debate had lived in Gwynedd for twenty years, and yet still pronounced it Gwin-ned. How many times in those twenty years had he heard the correct pronunciation of the county he lived in? And how many times must he have thought, 'No, I'm going to keep calling it Gwin-ned? It's only bonkers nationalists who call it by that silly Welsh name.' Prat. People like him are only in Wales because they can't afford Dorset or Devon. Lucky Dorset and Devon.

The Welsh language is one of the greatest assets, not just of Wales, but of Britain and Europe. Its survival, and even modest resurgence, is a wonderful testimony to the power of something very human, in often very trying circumstances. Despite the centuries of attempted official murder of the language, despite the fact that it has lived next door to the most expansionist language and culture the world has ever seen, it is still with us, it is moreover widely spoken throughout much of Wales, and it sustains a huge variety of cultural life. Even for the most determined of monoglot English speakers, who have been able to inculcate a fifty percent blindness to all flashes of bilingualism, there is a growing realisation that they cannot completely ignore Cymraeg, even if they try. And, boy, do they try.

Blanket bilingualism, however, is an easy – and sometimes justified – target. We should hope that the growing confidence in Wales enables us to jettison some of the more ridiculous examples, when communication can resemble an everlasting Eurovision Song Contest, with every last word being spoken breathlessly, in two languages, packed in cheek-by-jowl. Perhaps, dare I suggest, Welsh may be allowed to be the sole language proffered, when the sense is utterly obvious? In evidence for this point of view, let me call up a sign on the M4 that sets my teeth on edge every time I pass it, pointing the way to:

Parc

Margam

Park

Go on, let's go wild and make the bold assumption that monoglot English speakers could work out just what Parc Margam might be. Next stop Banc Barclays Bank.

Chapter 3

THE RUBBISH OF CREATION:
The Welsh Landscape

*Anyway, it was Wales all right... There was no obvious giveaway,
like road signs in two languages or closed-down factories, but
something was there, an extra greenness in the grass, a softness
in the light, something that was very like England and yet not
England at all, more a matter of feeling not seeing but not just
feeling, something run-down and sad but simpler and freer than
England all the same.*

Kingsley Amis, *The Old Devils*, 1986

Whether it's done by road, railway, bridge or footpath, you can almost always tell when you've crossed the border from England into Wales. The contours get sharper, the greens deeper and the crags that little bit sulkier; there's no doubt that you're crossing into another land and another dimension. For many visitors, this has been a cause for wonder and pleasure, and has brought them back time and again. For a sizeable number, however, these very differences, in both physical landscape and the feeling of the place, kick off feelings of incomprehension that can quickly turn into haughty disdain or vitriolic dismissal. And very many observers have quickly made the connection between the seemingly wild, inhospitable landscape and the characteristics of its inhabitants. The tone was set way back in the twelfth century, when King Henry II wrote to the Emperor of Byzantium that, 'The Welsh are a wild people who cannot be tamed.' But it never stopped them trying.

Few populations are deemed to be as inextricably linked

to their physical landscape as the Welsh. Even amongst the nations of the British Isles, Wales stands out as the one whose national characteristics are most shaped by its natural environment, most notably as a highland country (some four-fifths of the landmass of Wales is upland). Even though there are many higher peaks in the Scottish Highlands, even Scotland escapes the same conflation of national character and physical terrain. After all, the vast majority of the Scottish population, as well as most of its industry and commerce, is found in the highly urbanised central Lowland belt between Glasgow and Edinburgh. The Highlands, a jewel of pride for any Scot, are for the most part a romantic backdrop, a distant place of escape and refuge, both emotional and physical. There is no such escape in Wales. The starkness of the physical terrain is ubiquitous. Even Wales' two largest cities, Cardiff and Swansea, are hemmed in by mountains, and its greatest non-city city, the sprawling spider conurbation of the Valleys, is entirely defined by the narrow strips of frantic urbanisation on the valley floor, sided by sheer slopes. Nowhere is far from the hills, and it's never forgotten on either side of the border.

It is a truth embedded in the collective consciousness of both the Welsh and the English, that Wales' mountainous nature directly fed its appetite and ability for rebellion. The early years of Owain Glyndŵr's uprising against Henry IV were beautifully co-ordinated, in terms of utilising both the landscape and climate of Wales to maximise his chances against a vastly wealthier and better-equipped opposition. Glyndŵr could retreat into his network of mountain hideaways, secure in the knowledge that the English troops would never find him. His big battle victories, such as at Hyddgen and Pilleth, in the early stages of his campaign, were won largely due to his strategy of using the landscape to his tactical advantage.

The contrast with England – and, in particular, the parts of England where money and power are most concentrated – could not be greater. All of the flatter regions of central, southern and eastern England are landscapes that have been utterly subjugated to the will and whim of man. It is a simple, crude fight; rational man versus irrational landscape; and in most of England, man has most definitely won. His will has prevailed in every last corner. Landscape, like a wild beast, has been tamed.

But not in Wales. The wild beast that is the Welsh landscape roars on, seemingly unchecked to amateur eyes. The dizzying contours, sudden dead-end valleys and sheer harshness of the terrain have forced man to live and build his infrastructure in far more humble ways, ways that can never disguise their ultimate fragility. If much of England offers a battle between man and landscape that man has been able to win, no-one in their right mind would try to take on the Welsh landscape and beat it. Man's only hope is to live along side it, to manage it, tame it around the edges as best he possibly can.

'The Very Rubbish of Noah's Flood'

Awesome, that much over-used word popularised by American pop culture, is the word for the Welsh landscape. And awe implies a certain amount of terror inherent within it. It's a terror that has often been noted by visitors from across the border. The tone was set by the first wave of English visitors in the seventeenth and eighteenth centuries. William Richards, in his tome *Wallography*, of 1682, established something of a precedent:

> *The land is mountainous and yields pretty handsome*
> *clambering for goats, and hath variety of precipices to break*
> *one's neck, which a man must do sooner than fill his belly, the*
> *soil being barren and an excellent place to breed famine in.*

Immediately, the link was made between the rawness of the landscape and the supposed rawness of the population and their life and prospects. For eighteenth-century visitors especially, leaving a Restoration, and later Georgian, world of rationalism and mannered elegance, it all came as a bit of a shock, and they wasted no time in declaiming loudly their horror. In 1740, Archbishop Thomas Herring described Wales as being 'like the rubbish of creation', words that allowed a rampant snobbery free rein. They were perhaps an echo of an earlier travelogue, written by one E B in 1700: *A Trip To North Wales*, where he described what he saw as 'the fag end of creation; the very rubbish of Noah's flood; the highest English hills are as cherrystones to the Welsh Alps, so that there is not in the whole world a people that live so near to and yet so far from heaven, as the Welsh do.'

And there it is again, any excuse to nail the perceived shortcomings of the Welsh as a race. If you saw the landscape as nothing more than debris and waste, just how low did that make the people who lived their lives on this spoil tip? Dehumanised, dirty, demonised, they were beyond salvation, quite literally. And if this was the result of their physical landscape, an utterly immovable factor, it also let the visitors off the hook of trying to do or say anything useful, generous or kind about it. They could, to corrupt that old shampoo ad slogan, just diss and go.

Perhaps the most famous of early eighteenth-century visitors was Daniel Defoe, whose 1724 book, *A Tour through the Whole Island of Great Britain* became something of a benchmark for travel writing in the decades to come. Hardly surprisingly, Wales horrified Defoe, who was a be-wigged and be-powdered devotee of the Age of Reason, the father of patrician English journalism and a fervent believer in mercantile trade. To him, beauty lay in smooth profitability and urbane elegance, qualities

Original cartoon: Toby Driver

ever lacking in Wales. Right at the outset of his account, he even regrets having ever come to Wales in the first place:

> ...indeed, we began to repent our Curiosity, as not having met anything worth the trouble; and a Country looking so full of horror, that we thought to have given over the Enterprise and have left Wales out of our Circuit.

To Defoe, the more Welsh a place was, the more it disgusted him. Caernarfon he called 'a good town', but only because it was 'with a castle built by Edward I to curb and reduce the wild people of the mountains, and secure the passage into Anglesea.' Of the island itself, he stated baldly that 'There is nothing of note to be seen in the Isle of Anglesea but the town, and the castle of Baumaris [sic], which was also built by King Edward I,' despite noting, with indifference, that the island was home to one of the greatest concentrations of ancient relics to be found in the whole of Britain. This included 'two circles of stones in that island, such as Stone-henge... but we did not go to see it.' When he did bother to check out Anglesey's unique neolithic heritage, he was singularly unimpressed by the fact that they were 'generally without any inscription, or regular shape or any mark, to intimate for who, or for what they were so placed.'

The only places that elicited anything like enthusiasm from Defoe were those that either reminded him most of England, or that seemed to offer any chance of profitable exploitation for English markets. Montgomery was described as 'a good fashionable Place,' largely thanks to the fact that it had 'many English dwelling in it.' Not surprisingly, he was particularly struck by southern Pembrokeshire:

> ...all this Part of Wales is a rich and flourishing Country, but especially this Part is so very pleasant, and fertile, and is so well cultivated, that 'tis called by Distinction, Little England beyond Wales.

You can almost hear the audible sigh of relief as his tour of Wales came to an end:

> We came to Denbeigh [sic] town. This is the county town, and is a large populous place, which carries something in its countenance of its neighbourhood to England, but that which was most surprizing, after such a tiresom and fatiguing journey, over the unhospitable mountains of Merioneth, and Carnarvonshire, was, that descending now from the hills, we came into a most pleasant, fruitful, populous, and delicious vale, full of villages and towns, the fields shining with corn, just ready for the reapers, the meadows green and flowery, and a fine river, with a mild and gentle stream running thro' it: Nor is it a small or casual intermission, but we had a prospect of the country open before us, for above 20 miles, in length, and from 5 to 7 miles in breadth, all smiling with the same kind of complexion; which made us think our selves in England again, all on a sudden.

'A Truly Fairy Place'

As the eighteenth century drew to a close, perceptions of the Welsh landscape started to change appreciably. The ever-increasing din of industrialisation was turning large swathes of England into blackened, crowded hell-holes. Furthermore, travel was fast becoming the occupation of the wealthy and privileged, and exposure to the peaks of Europe – the Alps in particular – had inculcated in many young Turks an appreciation of mountainous terrain and its terrific beauty. In the aftermath of the French Revolution of 1789, with Europe in

Cavern Cascade, Hafod, Ceredigion. While the nearby hills were being blasted for mineral extraction, Thomas Johnes of Hafod was dynamiting his estate to provide a better view for his genteel guests. The most startling example can still be seen today, in the tunnel blasted out of the rock to afford a vista over a waterfall.
Photo: author

political turmoil, the Grand Tour of the continent waned, and English gentry instead turned their gaze towards the wilder parts of the Lake District, Scotland and Wales for their fix of upland loveliness. Landscape artists, in particular, began to flock to Wales in pursuit of the perfect painting, usually laden with classical allegory and featuring austere crags topped by romantic ruins alongside churning rivers and waterfalls. Between 1770 and 1815, over eighty books appeared detailing gentrified tours in Wales.

Thus was born the Picturesque, first named by an English cleric, the Reverend William Gilpin in his 1782 book, *Observations on the River Wye, and Several Parts of South Wales Relative Chiefly to Picturesque Beauty*. Before long, the Picturesque wasn't merely a theory of composition in painting, but an entire lifestyle, available for those wealthy and indulgent enough to pursue it. Perhaps the greatest-known example in Wales of the Picturesque writ large was the Hafod estate, near Pontrhydygroes, in Ceredigion, developed by Thomas Johnes, an adherent of the theory, from the 1780s onwards. George Borrow, when he visited the estate in 1854, found the house 'A truly fairy place... beautiful but fantastic'.

The house, in much decay, was finally torn down in 1959, although recent years have seen the accompanying estate at Hafod being restored to something of its former glory. Its well worth seeing, if only to get a handle on the theories of the Picturesque and how they were applied in open-air, three-dimensional splendour. Raw nature is not good enough for the Picturesque. It must be tweaked, fiddled with and framed, in order to satisfy its fussy devotees – framed even quite literally. It was not unheard of for Picturesque designers to carry around with them an empty picture frame, which they could hold up, in order to work out how nature needed to be altered to satisfy the proportions of a picture. The Hafod estate is littered with fancy little follies and artificial viewpoints, rivers and streams were re-coursed and thrown over false waterfalls, in order to better satisfy the composition.

A Picturesque estate is like a 3D version of a winsome landscape painting, the sort that clogs up every provincial art gallery in the land. It is perhaps the first example of Virtual Reality.

These two distinct strands of English thought about the Welsh landscape – as either the 'fag end of creation', or a marvel of the Picturesque – have endured to this day. Most commentators seem to have fallen down on one side or the other. At first glance, the two perspectives seem to be in stark opposition to each other, although, as with so many opposites, they are perhaps more like two sides of the same coin, for both are based on a very superficial reading of the Welsh landscape. As always, *la verité est entre les deux*; the truth lies between the two.

Scraping the Bottom of the Barren

To the 'fag end of creation' point of view there have been many subscribers, since Victorian times. Whereas pre-industrial travellers tended to focus on the bleak terror of the country's rocky crags, once the industrial revolution had roared into being, it was the Valleys and the slate quarries of north Wales that most stunned and horrified visiting commentators – and, to be fair, there must have been plenty to be horrified by. Now that we no longer really mine or make anything, sneers about the Welsh landscape usually manifest themselves in predictable guide book pot-shots at some very easy targets; namely, tatty old seaside resorts and the like. I've been unable to resist them myself – sometimes the goal is just too wide and inviting not to lob an easy ball into. It was, after all, my very own *Rough Guide to Wales* that used to begin its account of Rhyl: 'Anything you can do in Rhyl, you can do better elsewhere,' a sentence that once caused me to be locked into the town's tourist office, while its manager harangued me for my meanness of spirit. The north Wales Costa Geriatrica is surely the easiest target in modern Wales, and there is a long list of writers who have tried to come up with new and novel ways of being utterly snotty about it. No one's managed to string together a better, or more devastatingly deadpan, slagging off than the peerless Bill Bryson:

> *From the train, north Wales looked like holiday hell – endless ranks of prison-camp caravan parks standing in fields in the middle of a lonely, wind beaten nowhere, on the wrong side of the railway line and a merciless dual carriageway, with views over a boundless estuary of moist sand dotted with treacherous-looking sinkholes and, far off, a distant smear of sea. It seemed an odd type of holiday option to me, the idea of sleeping in a tin box in a lonesome field miles from anywhere in a climate like Britain's and emerging each morning with hundreds of other people from identical tin boxes, crossing the rail line and dual carriageway and hiking over a desert of sinkholes in order to dip your toes in a distant sea full of Liverpool turds. I can't put my finger on what exactly, but something about it didn't appeal to me.*
>
> Notes from a Small Island, 1998

In many ways, taking the piss out of Rhyl or Colwyn Bay, Barry Island or Benllech, is a relatively safe way of venting your spleen. After all, these sort of places have long been abandoned to the tourist shilling, so that having a go at them does not necessarily mean that you are, *ipso facto*, having a go at Wales. The landscape and the culture have long been divorced, so no danger of causing much offence, other than to the poor sods whose Stygian task it is to manage the Rhyl tourist office.

This is a distinctly recent change, for many an earlier lambasting of the Welsh landscape did not hesitate to extrapolate the view into a far wider, and far more savage, critique of Wales as a nation and the Welsh as a race. Over the years, the editorial columns of the London papers have provided many fine examples of bombastic anti-Welsh sentiment. This example, from *The Times* of September 1866, went into purple-prosed overdrive as it considered the paucity of the Welsh landscape and what they decided it therefore told the world about the people who lived there:

> *Wales, it should be remembered, is a small country, unfavourably situated for commercial purposes, with an indifferent soil, and inhabited by an unenterprising people. It is true it possesses valuable minerals but these have been chiefly developed by English energy and for the supply of English wants. A bare existence on the most primitive food of a mountainous race is all that the Welsh could enjoy if left to themselves.*

Yet again, there is a subliminal image of a feral race, more animal than human, eking out the most meagre of existences in this supposedly barren land. Yet again, the Welsh are to be considered by their English neighbours as less human and less evolved. That way, of course, it matters not if they are treated like dogs if they're lucky, vermin if they're not.

It is this supposed barrenness of Wales that repeatedly crops up like a *leitmotif* in English observations. In a largely upland country, it is incontrovertibly true that much of the land is unsuitable for crop growing or animal pasture. Wales, however, is blessed with some plentifully fertile areas: not for nothing was the island of Anglesey, a rolling green pastureland, known as *Mam Cymru*, the Mother of Wales, and supplier of crops to the rest of the country. Very much of the south-western counties of Ceredigion, Carmarthenshire and Pembrokeshire is similarly green and lush, as are huge swathes of inland Powys, Monmouthshire, Denbighshire and Flintshire. Stand on top of

Near Abergynolwyn, Gwynedd.
Photo: author

the Snowdonia outcrops of Yr Eifl and you gain a fabulous view over the verdant patchwork of fields and farms that is the Llŷn peninsula. Taken as a whole, Wales is most definitely not a barren land; there is ample good farming opportunity to satisfy the needs of a country of less than three million people, with plenty to spare. To write it off as barren and inhospitable is geographical gerrymandering of the slyest kind.

But still the descriptions of a knackered and impotent landscape keep rolling in. In modern times, the profusion of spoil-heaps and waste from the mining and quarrying industries have only added fuel to this particularly stubborn fire. The irony there, of course, is that these very spoil-heaps, looming large over the Valleys of Glamorgan or the slate towns of Gwynedd, are, in the main, the by-products of industries that came and went with ferocious speed and which failed miserably to clear up after themselves, and that, almost without exception, these were industries owned and driven by English lords and landowners. Instead of contextualising the rusty ruins as yet another form of exploitation of Wales, its natural resources and its people, they have been used as a stick with which to beat the country. Damned if you do, damned if you don't.

Even a terrible disaster such as the one that happened at Aberfan in October 1966, only briefly brought the real culprits into the frame. The horror awoken world-wide by the death of 28 adults and 116 children, buried under an obscene avalanche of coal sludge, was dissipated by nervous National Coal Board officials and government ministers, eager to deflect the blame. Dennis Potter hit the nail on the head in the immediate aftermath of Aberfan, when he wrote

> ...the disgust that such gargantuan waste should have been piled at people's backyards. Why should it be? Why is it thought necessary to be so loathsomely uncivilised? And when the anger of this tragedy has left the front pages, there is still more and yet more to be angry about for a place and a people like this.

The late Gwynfor Evans, then the newly-elected first Plaid Cymru MP, put the tragedy in even sharper focus, when he said in the House of Commons, 'Let us suppose that such a monstrous mountain had been built above Hampstead or Eton, where the children of the men of power and wealth are at school...' But that, of course, could never have happened. No community in the wealthier parts of England would ever have been treated with such callous disregard. It was the Welsh working-class, a people regularly portrayed in the London media as almost sub-human, who were deemed ultimately expendable.

'Most Sublimely Terrible'

To those of an incurably Picturesque or Romantic point of view, Wales has been a significant magnet since the tail end of the eighteenth century. This topic, specifically with regard to those who have re-located permanently to Wales, is explored further in the chapter entitled The Good Life, but in the context of landscape and visitors, it has loomed ever large. First off the bus was that pair of old hippies, Wordsworth and Coleridge, lah-lahing their way through the mountainous scenery and getting lost in their own misty reverie.

William Wordsworth and Samuel Taylor Coleridge form one of the enduring comedy double acts of English literature. Like all such acts, they comprised the straight man and the fall guy. Wordsworth, prim, proper and poetic, was the straight one. Coleridge, usually ripped to the tits on fine opiates, served as his extravagant foil. It's no surprise that Wordsworth's winsome doggerel, all daffodils and rustic characters leaning on creaky gates, has ended up printed on tea towels and souvenir tins of shortbread. Coleridge's darker, denser, druggier ramblings are the stuff of a far more intense mind. When it came to Wales, Wordsworth managed a few whimsical rhymes, most famously, his take on Tintern Abbey ('How oft, in spirit, have I turned to thee/O sylvan Wye! thou wanderer thro' the woods/How often has my spirit turned to thee!'), while Coleridge raged and raved and howled at the moon. To him, the wildness of the Welsh landscape inflamed and massaged his own wild passions. On one trip, in summer 1794, he used the scenery to wallow in, as a way of getting over some romantic heartbreak, and found it the perfect cure: 'I have been wandering among the wild-wood scenery and terrible Graces of the Welsh mountains to wear away the Images of the past!' he wrote to his friend Henry Martin. Sounding uncannily like a Vincent Price character in some Hammer horror shlockbuster, the landscape, to him, was '...most sublimely terrible... it surpasses everything I could have conceived.'

If the poets were around today, Wordsworth would be one of those anaemic hippies, flogging home-made greetings cards at Machynlleth or Cardigan market. Coleridge, however, like something straight from the page of Aberystwyth novelist Niall Griffiths, would be one of the drug-fuelled furies, rampaging through the mountains and moors of mid Wales, before pitching head-first into a week-long binge. Of all the contemporary takes by English writers on the Welsh landscape, it is those of Griffiths, originally from Liverpool, which most thrillingly hit the mark. For him, and for Coleridge and others before him, the contours of Wales are vividly alive, places that shout and hum and throb with a morbid intensity that not everyone is able – or willing – to appreciate. In marked contrast to the many English visitors who have looked and seen only rubble and barren waste, Griffiths has looked and let the scene assault every one of his senses. It is a relationship of passion – so much so, indeed, that heartbreak is only ever just around the corner.

In his novels, *Grits* and *Sheepshagger*, Niall Griffiths allows the Welsh landscape to be the major character: always there, framing everything, controlling, dictating, cajoling. His deeper attitude to the physical country is in marked contrast to earlier Romantics, many of whom were able to appreciate the stark beauty, but only as a living painting. Griffiths, and other contemporary observers, have at last detected the cultural contexts woven into the landscape, so that the beauty comes hand-in-hand with the melancholy of a marginalised culture. Some might argue that George Borrow was the first English writer to make the link, although it's often hard to detect in his bombastic approach. Certainly, Griffiths' fusion of landscape and personal powerlessness harks back more to the full-blooded prose and poetry of indigenous Welsh language writers like T H Parry-Williams, Bobi Jones and Caradog Pritchard.

To the more romantic view of the Welsh landscape, there has never been any shortage of subscribers, since Wordsworth. All too often, however, the view of the country as a 3D postcard demands quite a sustained effort to exclude all of the social, economic and cultural contexts that are threaded through it. It seems that many incomers into rural Wales manage this really quite difficult feat. To them, it's the view that matters more than anything else, and, like the proponents of the Picturesque two centuries before, they frame their view like a wall-mounted photograph of something pretty, something lovely but something, ultimately, only to look at, to impress your friends with, but not to engage with.

The Living Postcard

The development of picture postcards over the past century or so tells us much about the Welsh landscape that is packaged and sold to visitors (and, by extension, many of those who, one sun-dappled day in Betws-y-Coed, decided to mutate from visitor to incomer). Hardly surprisingly, it's an industry in Wales that has long been geared towards English perceptions, as it is English people who continue to make up the vast majority of those who come to Wales as tourists. Postcards, in the early days, at the tail end of the nineteenth century, were largely of popular tourist sights, particularly natural features such as waterfalls and mountain passes, framed and clipped in the best traditions of the Picturesque.

During the picture postcard's heyday, in the Edwardian

period of the early twentieth century, new strains of postcard became very popular. While the natural beauty spots and seaside resort cards continued to flourish, humorous cartoon cards became a modish alternative. In Wales, there seemed endless lame jokes made in these cards (illustrated in Chapters 1 and 2) regarding the Welsh language, and particularly the difficulty in pronouncing place names, as well as cartoon cards of the crassest Welsh stereotypes.

Twenty or thirty years ago, the only postcards you could get were shocking things, the hideous hangover of post-war, knees-up, holiday fun. Colours were lurid, subjects were cheesy and obvious, and there seemed to be a law that demanded the representation of at least one cheery family in every shot. Fair enough when the shot was of the crazy golf course at Butlins, Pwllheli, but slightly more contrived when it was of, say, a magnificent mountain pass, and the only way of wedging the Postcard Family into the scene was to have them grouped by the side of the road around their (bright orange) Austin Allegro.

Three photographers revolutionised the Welsh postcard scene in the 1980s and early 1990s. Dave Newbould (Origins), Janet Baxter (Cymric Cards) and Jeremy Moore (Wild Wales) are all superb landscape photographers, specialising in staggering, epic shots of Welsh mountains, rivers, lakes and beaches, all suffused in gorgeous, golden light, or the shuddering pinks of sunrise and sunset. Rarely are the wonders of nature in these cards ruined by anything man-made or, even worse, by people themselves. This is photography as luscious landscape porn and it has sold by the truckload.

The three photographers who have now got the Welsh postcard (plus notelet, calendar and greetings card) market by the very picturesque short and curlies share similar histories, in that they are all English, and came to Wales between twenty and thirty years ago. The Wales that they are photographing so brilliantly is largely English Wales, a land of startling physical prowess but with no evident cultural depth. Compare this work with the portfolios of native Welsh photographers like Marian Delyth or Ron Davies (not that one), much of whose subject matter also concerns the landscape of Wales. On their photos, there is muck, mud, rust and rain amidst the grandeur. The landscape is real, profound, complicated, heartbreaking and unmistakeably Welsh. It does not sell many postcards to tourists.

Chapter 4

THE CELTIC FRINGE:
Wales at the Margins

Wales: *see England.*

Encyclopaedia Britannica, 1888

Despite the limited devolution package that was granted to Scotland and Wales in the wake of Tony Blair's 1997 election victory, Britain remains one of the Western world's most centralised nation-states. The United Kingdom of Great Britain and (Northern) Ireland was explicitly created in 1801 as a product of, and engine for, the industrial, military and colonial age, functions it has unswervingly fulfilled ever since. London was its beating heart and from there came all government, opinion, attitude, press and power. Everywhere out of the south-east of England was also out of the loop, and it has been impossible to right this imbalance as yet, such is its deep-rootedness in our recent history. Although it is true that Birmingham, Bradford and Blackpool have rightly felt ostracised and patronised by this tendency, particular extremes of marginalisation have been dished out to the 'Celtic Fringe' (a name which gives itself magnificently away), and none more so than to Wales. The idea that Wales is remote, inaccessible, a mere coat-tail to something bigger and better has underpinned so much thinking that it has become a truism, without ever actually being inherently true.

It does, of course, entirely depend on where you place the

The last stone fortresses in Britain, the roundhouses of Nantyglo were constructed in 1816 by the English ironmasters Joseph and Crawshay Bailey. They were trying, yet again, to cut their workers' wages and feared armed insurrection. The roundhouses, with their four foot thick walls and iron doors with musket holes, were where they planned to hole up in case things became too hot to handle.

Photo: author

centre. If London – tucked away in the very south-eastern corner of this island – is to be considered as the hub of everything, then, yes, of course, Wales becomes, by definition, marginal. If Wales is only looked at in English terms, and south-eastern English terms at that, then it is fit only for whatever detritus subsequent London governments have dreamed up for the fringes of the kingdom. Out of sight and well and truly out of mind. But London being the epicentre of everything is only an artificial construct, the product of human politicking, industrialisation, various Acts of Union and belligerent imperialism. Go back a millennium and a half, when sea travel was the main method of transport, and the links between the Celtic countries were at their strongest, and Wales – particularly the west coast – would have been the hub of its day; St David's, say, the Birmingham New Street of its time. It's just a matter of perspective, not inalienable fact.

As ever, writer Jan Morris captured this tendency with her characteristic deftness of touch. Describing the first leg of a drive from her home in north-west Wales to Montenegro, in the Balkans (in the essay *Not So Far: A European Journey*), she wrote

> *It is as though the British Isles are tilted permanently to one corner – the south-east corner, bottom right, where London stands seething upon the Thames. Everything slithers and tumbles down there, all the talent, all the money, and when I got on to the M4 motorway that morning I felt that I was being swept away helter-skelter, willy-nilly across the breadth of England. Around me all the energies of the place seemed to be heading in a single direction – the trucks from Cornwall and South Wales, the tourist buses, the ramshackle No Nuclear estate cars, the stream of expense-account Fords, their salesmen drivers tapping their steering wheels to the rhythm of Radio One. London! London! shouted the direction signs. London! screamed the blue and white train, streaking eastwards beside the road, and when I turned off to the south and made for Dover, still I felt the presence of the capital tugging away at me, as it tugs the commuters from their mock-Tudor villas day after day from the far reaches of Surrey and pastoral Hampshire.*

These centripetal forces that propel all down to the south-east are not an inevitable, inescapable fact of geography. If the centre is relocated, to more accurately reflect the reality of the topography and anthropology of the British Isles, hitherto marginalised parts of the country suddenly find themselves much nearer the lifeblood, the pulse of the nation. This is part of the theory behind devolution, or in that much-vaunted word from John Major's days in government, subsidiarity, the idea that decisions should be taken at the level of government that is as close as possible to the people they will affect.

The limited devolution that Wales has finally won seems to have had little effect yet in countering the centuries of marginalisation. There is an inescapable feeling that the kernel of power (and not much power at that) has moved only from south-east England to south-east Wales. To continue Jan Morris' imagery, these islands are very skewed to the bottom right. Just look at a map of Britain and Ireland. At every turn, power, money and authority slide down to the south and east. Each capital city – Dublin, Belfast, Cardiff, Edinburgh and London – is in the east, and usually the south, too, of its patch. The west, in particular, and the north, to some extent, are considered to be the lunatic fringe and are treated accordingly.

Never Mind the Royals

It's a tendency that is graphically illustrated by that most glittering symbol of imperial Britishness, the royal family. All it takes is a swift look at where they choose to live. The royal map has its southern bulwarks (Buckingham Palace in London, Windsor Castle), its easterly hideout (Sandringham in Norfolk) and its northerly outposts (Holyrood in Edinburgh and Victoria's favourite, the grim and grey Balmoral in the Dee Valley of north-east Scotland). One compass point – the west – is conspicuously absent from the Windsors' long list of forwarding addresses. On the rare occasions that Charles, the Prince of Wales, deigns to stay the night in his fiefdom, he used to opt (before an unseemly row about his sleeping arrangements prior to making a decent woman out of Camilla) for a guest bedroom at Powis Castle, near Y Trallwng, Welshpool, just spitting distance from the English border. There had been some talk of recognising Powis as royalty's official Welsh palace, but it never came to much. After all, it's hardly a pressing concern, either for the royal family, or, indeed, for Wales. Fittingly, the nearest thing on Welsh soil to a modern royal residence is an overgrown railway siding at Portskewett, at the Welsh end of the Severn Tunnel, where visiting royals would get their beauty sleep before progressing deep into unknown territory. Resting their expensive heads in an hermetically-sealed mobile palace was obviously infinitely preferable to any of the hotels, castles, or stately homes of Wales.

In modern times, no member of the royal family has ever kept a house in this country, although a recent announcement has made us believe that this is about to change. In these media-savvy times, and after the fallout from his bust-up with Powis Castle, there had been some talk of Prince Charles buying a Welsh base, and in November 2006 it was announced that he (or rather his office, the Duchy of Cornwall) was about to purchase Llwynywormwood, a 192-acre estate near Llandovery, Carmarthenshire. The spin was that this was to be the Welsh base for Charles and Camilla, but it's hard to imagine them plus staff squeezed into a three-bedroom farmhouse. The estate's true vocation will be as an organic farm, with an assortment of holiday cottage accommodation. That said, Charles is a good deal more enthusiastic about his 'principality' than many of his predecessors. Of the twenty previous English heir-to-the-thrones entitled Prince of Wales since the infant Edward II in 1302, fewer than half of them ever bothered to even visit the land that gave them their title.

In sharp contrast to their enthusiasm for tartan, porridge and Highland Games, the royals have never tried to appropriate on any substantial level any of the paraphernalia of Welshness, save perhaps for the corgis and Prince Charles' hilarious, occasional forays into Cymraeg. When it came to Charles' eldest, Prince William, choosing a university, he opted immediately – and very unsurprisingly – for deeply Establishment St Andrews, in Scotland, saying that he wasn't coming to Wales because, if all goes to plan and he becomes the Prince of Wales when his old man gets the top job, he'd be seeing plenty of us in the future. Yeah, right. Otherwise, I'm sure he'd have been zipping off to Lampeter quicker than you could say Special Branch Protection.

If the royals think of Wales at all, it is most likely in the same way that you'd think of a persistent itch: hard to get shot of, needs paying a bit of attention and occasionally flares up into something really annoying. So Wales gets occasional pantomimes, like the 1969 Investiture in Caernarfon, or 21-gun salutes as the Queen opens the Senedd in Cardiff, but they're mere away-days for the royals, before they scuttle quickly back across the border. Sometimes, that is even quicker than planned: to this day, Aberystwyth remains the only place in the world where, in all her half-century on the throne, the Queen has had to cut short a visit due to protestors. To them, it's a disgrace. To many in Wales, it's a source of national pride.

Wood, Wind and Water

Once a place has been so thoroughly and so effectively marginalised, it makes it very easy to do absolutely anything unpleasant to it. Almost every corner of Wales is laden with features that shout and scream it to be a landscape that has been left – indeed, perhaps, *encouraged* – to rot as a distant, marginal concern, scarcely to be bothered with. There are many examples of this, from the fighter jets screaming over villages and valleys, to the abandoned quarries and mines that

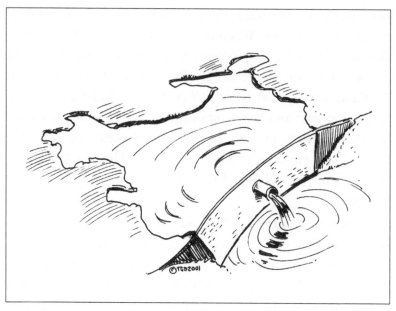

Original cartoon: Toby Driver

pock the landscape like festering sores.

I recently hiked over the Tarren mountain range, a ridge of peaks to the south of Cader Idris and only a slate's throw from my front door. It was a gloriously sunny bank holiday weekend, yet I walked for eight hours and met no-one else all day. The landscape is a classic marginalised one, condemned as being way out on the periphery, despite being absolutely magical and almost the geographical heart of Wales. Coming down off the highest peak, Tarren-y-Gesail, gave me a view that perfectly symbolised the progressive exploitation of the landscape. In the immediate foreground was an abandoned slate quarry, great shards of sharp spoil pointing in all directions amongst roofless huts and rusted winding gear. Behind that was a beautifully-shaped hill, cloaked by a tight cap of fast-growing conifers, leaving not one inch of space, sunlight or real nature between them. Behind that were hills dotted with whirring wind turbines, the latest incarnation of the long-standing belief that this wild, wonderful landscape is merely something to be ruthlessly exploited, that it has no inherent value of its own for anything other than what can be ripped from it, or imposed upon it.

While there have been good reasons for planting some conifers in Wales' more remote parts, the angular giants of the Forestry Commission have been allowed to run riot over huge swathes of the country. A clearer symbol of rural subjugation and marginalisation it would be hard to find. They are 'green concrete', nature at its most unnatural, choking to a swift and relentless death everything that once grew beneath them. Even when the trees are felled, there's nothing but a desolate wasteland left behind. The Forestry tracks thrust through them are like dusty motorways, obliterating ancient paths and rights of way in an instant. Every now and again, you'll stumble across the heartbreaking remains of an old farmhouse, once a crucible of small-scale, sustainable agriculture and Welsh culture, now roofless and forlorn, its occupants forcibly evicted when the men from the ministry came knocking. Small wonder that many Welsh commentators have looked at the ruler-straight lines of these plantations and seen not just a physical decimation, but an economic and cultural one too:

> *Fforest lle bu ffermydd...*
> *Ac yn y tywyllwch yn ei chanol hi*
> *Y mae ffau'r Minotawros Seisnig...*
>
> Forest where there used to be farms...
> And in the darkness in the middle of it
> Is the den of the English Minotaur.
>
> 'Gwenallt' (David Gwenallt Jones, Pontardawe)
> translation by the author

And now we have the wind turbines. Again, there are many

good reasons for rural Wales shouldering some responsibility for renewable energy, but it threatens to get out of hand. These monsters are marching across the hills of Wales like the most determined of invading armies, ripping up ancient landscapes and industrialising them, causing huge amounts of secondary noise and disruption and blighting views for mile upon mile. Wales, with 8.5% of the UK's total landmass and around 5% of the UK's population, is home to almost 50% of the UK's wind turbines. And there are proposals for many, many more, including a new breed of super-turbines, each one over 400 feet high. This new abuse of the landscape is a distinct echo of the reservoirs that have flooded rural Wales over the last century and a half.

Welsh political and cultural life was galvanised and changed utterly by the campaign about the Tryweryn valley of Meirionydd in the late 1950s and early 1960s. For a century, vast tracts of rural Wales had been flooded with impunity, to provide drinking water for the large industrial cities of England. A plaque, provided by the Liverpool Corporation, at Llyn Efyrnwy, Lake Vyrnwy, amply demonstrates the macho arrogance with which such tasks were undertaken; it celebrates the 'Taking and impounding of the waters of the Rivers Vyrnwy, Marchnant and Cowny.' It makes no mention of the fact that a village of four hundred inhabitants was drowned in the process, nor, for that matter, that 44 men died in the construction of the dam.

But Liverpool was thirsty for more, and in the 1950s the Corporation's attention turned to the River Tryweryn, running through a remote valley on the eastern flanks of the Migneint mountain range near Bala in Meirionydd. Remote Tryweryn may be, but it was not deserted. Hill farms abounded, a railway line ran through it, two stations served the scattered community and the village of Capel Celyn at its heart. Despite the opposition of

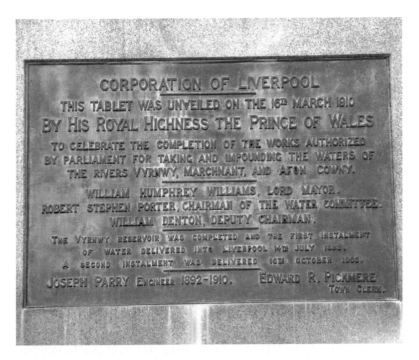

The plaque at Lake Vyrnwy: Impounding the water.
Photo: author

every Welsh local authority and almost every Welsh Member of Parliament, despite the protests, marches and petitions, the valley was flooded to provide water that, as it transpired, Liverpool never really needed and was able to sell on, instead, at a profit. Tryweryn remains to this day the starkest example of the sentiment expressed by R S Thomas in his poem, *Reservoirs*:

> *There are places in Wales I don't go,*
> *Reservoirs that are the subconscious*
> *Of a people, troubled far down*
> *With gravestones, chapels, villages even;*
> *The serenity of their expression*
> *Revolts me, it is a pose*
> *For strangers, a watercolour's appeal*
> *To the mass, instead of the poem's*

Harsher conditions. There are the hills,
Too; gardens gone under the scum
Of the forests; and the smashed faces
Of the farms with the stone trickle
Of their tears down the hills' side.

If R S Thomas was writing the poem today, I would like to think that the scarring, ghostly wind turbines would be added to the accusing list of glassy reservoirs, 'the scum of the forests' and the 'smashed faces of the farms', for they are all symptoms of a common malaise. And that malaise is the belief, expounded so often that it has become a self-propagating truth, that most of Wales – all of Wales, in fact, save for the south-eastern and north-eastern corners – is right out on the margins of civilisation. Allow that thought to take hold and it allows Wales to become a land written off as effectively useless. Staying with poetry, though as far removed from R S Thomas as could possibly be found, it should be left to the wondrous Harri Webb to sum up this malaise: 'We're looking up England's arsehole/Waiting for the manna to fall.'

At least the Tryweryn protests galvanised enough passion to ensure that similar schemes would be much more closely scrutinised – and resisted – in future. In 1970, a public enquiry was established to look at a scheme, proposed by the Severn River Authority, to drown the Dulas valley between Llanidloes and Rhayader, on the border of Montgomeryshire and Radnorshire, and home to some five hundred people. For the first time, and as a direct result of the Tryweryn campaign, factors other than the strictly economic were taken into consideration. These included the value of community life, the strength of culture and the human effects of transplanting so many people whose links had grown up over centuries. The enquiry came down against yet another reservoir, the scheme was scrapped and the community still thrives in its lush, beautiful valley.

Real-life paintballing fun in the Pembrokeshire National Park.
Photo: author

Bang, Bang, You're Dead

The might of the armed forces, however, is much harder to resist. Perhaps the worst culprit in Wales' marginalisation has been Britain's vast military machine. Polite public enquiries are nothing to the Army or the Air Force. The National Interest card is played, critics are silenced, and the needs of the boys with their flashy toys are paramount. Wales has long been the place to build Prisoner of War camps, construct air bases and shooting ranges, stockpile lethal arsenals and nuclear waste, and fly ear-splitting super-jets. How little Welsh culture counts to the military was most famously illustrated in the 1936 case of the Penyberth bombing school, on the Llŷn peninsula. The site was the government's third choice. Its first one, in Dorset, was spared because of the effect it would have on the local bird population. The second, in Northumberland, was turned down, also on conservation grounds, after a vocal campaign in *The Times* newspaper. The fact that the Penyberth scheme necessitated the demolition of an ancient Welsh plas, with connections to Owain Glyndŵr and beyond, counted for nothing. The Prime Minister, Stanley Baldwin, refused even to meet a deputation from Llŷn to discuss it. The house was demolished and the bombing school erected. To the London government, a hugely important plas, the living Welsh language, and community culture were nowhere near as important as Dorset birds or Northumberland flowers and stones. Ironically, the bombing school was regularly rendered useless, thanks to the district's renowned sea fogs that roll in regardless even of British government diktats.

It didn't stop there. Huge tracts of some of Wales' most beautiful landscape have been appropriated wholesale by the military. There can be no more poignant symbols of that than the ghostly, abandoned village of Flimston, part of the huge Castlemartin army range in south Pembrokeshire, where signs everywhere around warn you not to leave the road lest you get blown up by a land mine. Or take the B4519 across the Mynydd Epynt, between Aberhonddu, Brecon and Llanfair-ym-Muallt, Builth Wells, where the signs command you to not even stop as you drive across what is now a vast army training and firing ground. It's hard not to, however, such is the savage beauty of the Epynt and the arresting sight of the old Drovers' Arms, mid way between Upper Chapel and Garth. The first time I saw the place – once warm and welcoming to the drovers heading across Wales to the markets of the Marches, then a blank, boarded-up wreck – I felt obliged to linger a moment and take it all in. Within two minutes of stopping the car, an army Land

Rover had come at me, lights flashing. Two squaddies emerged, rifles slung casually across their shoulders, to give me the third degree as to who I was and what I was doing there (the fact that I was jotting down a few notes in my notebook didn't help matters), before forcibly pointing me on my way with the barrels of their guns. The fact that, in the 2001 Foot and Mouth Disease crisis, the Epynt was once again fingered as the place to burn and bury diseased carcasses of 40,000 animals, polluting local waterways and the air alike, shows how, once a place has been marginalised and turned into a huge tip, it is only ever likely to remain so. The Ministry of Defence always

Llyn Brianne, Carmarthenshire. Flooded valley, tick. Conifer plantations, tick. Army flight path, tick. Wind turbines, coming soon.
Photo: author

give glib assurances to local communities that, once they have finished in an area, they will leave it as they found it. Would that it could ever be the case. It never has been, and it never will be.

The tale of the Epynt – one of Wales' last wilderness areas, and, until its forcible clearance in 1940, a bastion of Welsh culture – is as representative of the military presence as anywhere in Wales. The army and government in London saw this sparsely-populated area as somewhere it would be monumentally easy to clear. They did not – and could not – see the invisible, but resolutely strong, ties and links between the fifty or so houses and farms, the chapel and the school and the pub, that were cleared, with the residents given but a few weeks to move. When the military personnel arrived to issue clearance notices, they even marched into the area's primary school and insisted on stating their unwelcome mission in front of a whole classroom of children – most of whom, perhaps thankfully, did not understand what they were being told by the staccato-voiced Englishman who had suddenly arrived in their class. People's recollections of the time all speak of more or less the same experience: particularly of the high-handedness with which the locals were treated.

I've recently filmed on the Epynt, crossing it on the small military road, with public access, from the village of Llywel across to Tirabad, near Llanymddyfri (Llandovery). It was a disheartening experience. In little more than sixty years, the place has been comprehensively cleared of its history and context, deracinated and turned into a blank, even hostile, mock battle ground. The semi-detached private company that now run the land on behalf of the MoD wanted £1500 off us just to cross their patch on a road that is marked as publicly accessible on maps (though after much pleading, they did reluctantly bring the price down to a mere five hundred quid). It's quite a money-making venture: not just the odd film crew, but the endless array of road rallies that use the range, all paying top dollar for the privilege. It's a far cry from the living that was being eked out on the same land by longstanding family farmers just a couple of generations ago.

The military are as rooted in the attitudes, politics and culture of Establishment Britain (for which, read England) as it is possible to be. It's no surprise that Wales, therefore, has seemed to be little more than a distant outpost viewed through the binoculars of their long-distance gaze. All too often, the country has been treated as some stroppy little imperial station, a mini Raj on the doorstep. A Royalist officer in the English Civil War of the mid seventeenth century pleaded with Charles I: 'If your Highness shall be pleased to command me to the Turk, or Jew, or Gentile, I will go on my bare feet to serve you, but from the Welsh, good Lord, deliver us.' Two centuries later, with the British Empire approaching its triumphalist zenith, a former Indian Army Officer, applying for the post of Chief Constable of Caernarfonshire, stated that he was well suited to the job, as, in India, he had served against the Hill Tribes of the Western Frontier. Punjab, Pwllheli – well, it's all the same, seen from the parade ground of Sandhurst: tetchy natives and tough terrain.

This imperial swagger has also allowed the military to crack down in Wales in ways that they would never have got away with in England. History is littered with fatal over-reactions by English soldiers against the faintest hint of trouble in Wales, including the troops that shot indiscriminately at a Chartist rally in Newport in 1839, killing over twenty demonstrators and sentencing the ringleaders to death, later commuted to transportation. By contrast, the mayor that ordered the random execution was knighted for his efforts. Merthyr Tydfil, the seething cauldron of a town that saw the first raising of the red flag, has been on the receiving end of more fatal military bullying than any other sprawl in Britain. But, as one Mrs Arbuthnot put it in her 1831 diary, when referring to a Merthyr incident:

> There has been a great riot in Wales and the soldiers have killed twenty-four people. When two or three were killed at Manchester, it was called the Peterloo Massacre and the newspapers for weeks wrote it up as the most outrageous and wicked proceeding ever heard of. But that was in Tory times; now this Welsh riot is scarcely mentioned.

Each of these ingredients – the reservoirs, the wind farms, the abandoned mines and quarries, the military zones, the dumps and the conifer plantations – are dispiriting enough in themselves. But it is inescapably true that they combine with such monotonous regularity in Wales as to leave in certain areas almost nothing else in the landscape. Taken together, it's hard to see them as anything less than a systematic and long-standing belittling of this beautiful, mineral-rich, potentially wealthy land (not, incidentally, as many contemporary English journalists would have it, the Albania of Western Europe, something it will only be if allowed to rot even further). It's not as if Wales is even allowed to benefit economically from the schemes imposed upon it. Despite the profusion of reservoirs, for example, and the even greater profusion of water that tumbles out of the sky on this western peninsula of Britain, water bills in Wales are still, on average, 17% higher than those in the areas of England to which the Welsh water is exported. Wales, on the edge of English consciousness, is unquestionably only seen as an adjunct to English needs.

Out of the Loop

All of the instruments of Britishness have served to marginalise Wales; it's not a question of difficult geography, but of aggressive politics. Transport is a notable case. It is often said, with some real justification, that, in transport terms, the Romans were the last to unite north and south Wales, through their great highway, Sarn Helen, which ran over 160 miles, from Carmarthen to near Conwy. Since then, almost all transport decisions have ignored the integrity of Wales as anything like a discrete unit. In the early nineteenth century, Wales was merely an inconvenient part of the route between London and Ireland, newly incorporated into the United Kingdom. It was a process that only continued apace with the arrival of the railways later that century. Railway mania swept the country from the 1840s onwards, with no central or social planning whatsoever. As a

"Two more Prime Ministers of emergent nations, Harold, demanding the usual . . ."

A hideous, doubly racist cartoon from 1968. In the light of Plaid Cymru's win in the 1966 Carmarthen by-election, and the Scottish National Party's victory a year later in Hamilton, the cartoonist looks forward ten years to independent Wales and Scotland joining the queue with their begging bowls to the London government. Recently emerged African nations are caricatured in the most base of ways.

By permission of *The Daily Express*

result, Wales ended up with a system of railways that served either traffic to Ireland (via Neyland, Pembroke, Fishguard and Holyhead), or that brought Welsh minerals to the booming metropolises of England. Either way, the end result was that main lines went only east-west, particularly the two tracks that ran along the north and south coasts. A century and a half later, we are still suffering with this legacy, for these remain the only really fast rail services in Wales. Twentieth-century road planning has merely replicated and exacerbated the problem, with the country's only two motorway-standard roads almost exactly mirroring the two fast rail lines. The building of a decent north-south highway in Wales has been a stated priority for governments since the 1920s. It still is.

Marginalisation is an inevitable by-product of lack of information, and, in this sphere too, Wales does not come off very well in the British context. The number of stories from Wales that feature in the London press, for example, is derisory. Ironically, in this age of devolution, it's a situation that has worsened in recent years, rather than improved. Thirty years ago, most of the British papers had dedicated Wales correspondents based here, who fed through stories to London on a regular basis. They have all gone, and coverage of Wales is left to various news and photo agencies, internet sources, or correspondents occasionally sent down here, but only if something blows up. You're more likely to see a property feature on 'bargain' Welsh houses in a London paper these days, than a real story from west of Offa's Dyke.

When they do bother to consider news from Wales, what ends up getting printed is frequently lamentable rubbish that displays a woeful command of the state of play here. After the 1997 devolution referendum just squeaked a victory for the Yes campaign, senior political journalist Peter Riddell wrote in *The Times*: 'It was the huge 'yes' vote in nationalist areas that turned the result.' Those 'nationalist areas' included such Plaid Cymru hotbeds as Swansea, Neath and Llandudno, it seems. When the controversy about my 2001 article 'Loaded Dice' in *Planet* hit the London papers, many of them managed to misread completely what I was saying, and turned it instead into something that suited their agenda much better. The *Daily Telegraph*, for instance, on its front page, had a four-column story headed 'English travel writer raises hackles in Wales.' It started: 'An English travel writer living in Wales is upsetting the people there with his views that it is a haven for "gun-toting crackpots". Not content with outing St David as a homosexual, Mike Parker says that the level of racism he has encountered in his new home has taken him by surprise.'

Sneaky. They managed to imply that my charge of racism was being levelled at Welsh people, when, in fact, it was explicitly aimed at those who had moved here as part of the 'white flight' from English cities. And to misreport an earlier piece that I'd written, where I'd said that the famously ascetic St David was doubtless celibate but should not necessarily be assumed to have been heterosexual, was a calculated move to increase the offence. I was away camping when this all blew up. On returning home, my telephone-answering machine was chock-full with requests for interviews from seemingly every local radio station in England. Almost all of them said something along the lines of, 'Can we do an interview with you about why you think the Welsh are so racist, please?' The *Mail on Sunday* rang me, to commission an article about this supposed racism of the Welsh (they hadn't read my original piece, of course, just the distorted newspaper reactions). When I said that I was attacking the racism of English people *in* Wales, rather than Welsh people, they quickly lost interest and cancelled the offer. It evidently didn't fit their script.

Centering Ourselves

'I would sooner go to hell than to Wales,' said Herbert Henry Asquith, in a 1905 House of Commons speech, three years before he was appointed Prime Minister of Wales, England, Scotland and Ireland. It's a sentiment that has been echoed by innumerable figures of the English Establishment, helped by the popular perception that as Wales is so far out on a limb, it's easy enough to treat it as a joke or an irrelevance. There are many echoes of the way Ireland was similarly dismissed by London politicians and royalty over the centuries. Geographically, of course, Ireland was dismissed as being even further out on the edge, portrayed as a distant rock on the very edge of civilisation. Go there now, and you'd never believe it. Eighty years of self-determination have allowed the Irish wholly to reposition the idea of where the centre of their identity lies. The distance from London matters not one jot, these days. In fact, Ireland uses its place on the western edge of the continent to maximum advantage, bridging the Atlantic between North America and Europe with aplomb and skill. Even in the twenty-five years that I've been travelling to Ireland, I have seen a revolution in its self-belief and sense of its own destiny. There's been a direct correlation with the lessening of ties with London, a loosening of the apron strings that had bound it for so long. And yet the physical position of Ireland has not changed one inch. In so many ways, it is a model for what Wales could – and should – do.

So strong has the marginalisation of Ireland, and Wales, been over the centuries that it's hardly surprising to see its pernicious effects rooted deep in the collective psyche of both countries. Perhaps the most extreme example can be found in the Unionist communities of Northern Ireland, surely the most tragic cultural grouping in these islands. Much as I loathe the politics of Ulster Unionism, you can't help but feel sorry for those stuck in this anomalous time warp of history, who can hardly be blamed for the fact that their ancestors were planted there four hundred years ago and have been told almost continually ever since that they were superior to their indigenous neighbours. Hearing them talk about 'the mainland' (ie Britain) is such a sad by-product of this strange history: 'the mainland' is what you'd expect someone on Skomer or Bardsey, Anglesey at a push, to call Wales, or Britain, not someone who lives on the twentieth largest island in the world, with an area of thirty-two and a half thousand square miles and a population of nearly six million.

In the British cultural sphere, so much of it emanating from London, it's all too easy to detect the same perspective still pulsing towards Wales. It happens so constantly, and so subtly, that anyone brought up in Britain takes it almost for granted. As is so often the case, it takes an outsider to see just how starkly this hopelessly skewed situation has arisen. Take Judith Isherwood, the Australian Chief Executive of the Wales Millennium Centre in Cardiff. When the centre first opened, she said in an interview: 'People are so rude about Wales. I can sometimes almost see people thinking our arts centre is just regional. It has been occupying my mind since I arrived. I said to someone the other day, "I never thought I would end up in Wales," and they said, "My dear, I do hope you don't end up in Wales." I was quite shocked they would say that. I had never been to Wales before, even though I had visited Britain several times, and I hadn't realised that when you cross the border it feels like a different country straight away, and that affects the psyche.'

I've experienced this withering attitude on the few occasions that I've written about Wales for the London press. If the piece doesn't include at least a few nods to the standard English clichés about Wales, the editor will almost invariably slide a few in without asking, so that – at best – the article comes out as a kind of identikit 'You thought it was all coal mines and sheep, but – surprise! – there's more to Wales than that these days.' A few years back, the *Independent on Sunday* teamed up with the Rough Guides, so that every week they got the author of a different book to write a 'best of' their patch, including a standard fact-box, with things like prices, climate and how to get there. When I came to write one for Wales, under 'How to get there', I wrote simply 'Go west'. After all, I thought, while it may well make sense to point people on to flight operators and the like when the destination under scrutiny was Hawaii or Thailand, it hardly worked quite the same for Wales in a British newspaper. The travel editor rang me immediately. 'Can't you put how much it costs to get the train from Paddington?' he said. 'So all your readers are in London, then?' I suggested. 'Er, I don't know,' he answered, blissfully unaware of any irony. 'Most of them, I think.' A pause. 'You know, I've never really considered it.' And he hasn't been alone in that.

Chapter 5

THE GOOD LIFE:
The English Invasion

Well, it looks like middle earth to me, then I would suggest that the rest of the people of Bethesda open their eyes – we live in the most beautiful place in the world. No drugs – just open them eyes wide.

'Bethesda Hippy', BBC website community notice board

Once, they came bearing swords and pikes. Now, they come armed with crystals and wind chimes. But is the result really very much less hostile? For centuries, Wales has been viewed with an earthy wistfulness by a certain section of the English population, who see in the smaller country a set of characteristics that they feel have been lost on their own side of the border.

You hear the mantras again and again: 'We wanted to escape the rat-race.' 'Moving here was like going back thirty years.' (Both quotations are from testimonies on a BBC website guide aimed at those moving to Wales.) Fuelled by the endless property'n'relocation bilge being poured out by the television companies and newspapers, it seems that half of England is in a state of nervous hypertension, cradling the ever-expanding value of their suburban pile, while excitedly eyeing the possibilities for a new life, a new start, that they hope it will afford them. The danger here is that, if too many people opt for the same thing as you, it can help destroy the very thing that attracted you in the first place.

COMPOST TOILETS? DEAR ME NO! ALL OUR TEEPEES HAVE FULL MAINS DRAINAGE, ELECTRICITY AND SATELLITE T.V!

Original cartoon: Toby Driver

In the early days, it was merely a physical attraction. As the industrial revolution spread its sooty way over vast swathes of England, the hunger for nature, beauty and wilderness began to draw artists and writers, eager to see the peaks of Snowdonia, or the waterfalls of central Wales (see the chapter The Welsh Landscape for more on this). For some, it has never gone beyond the merely physical; there are many English visitors and residents in Wales who absolutely love the landscape of the country, but who are scathing, or wholly disinterested, when it comes to looking at any of the cultural factors inextricably sewn into that landscape.

To many English people, however, these cultural contexts are just as fascinating as the physical beauty of the country, and there has been a steady stream of English pilgrims over the border to examine them. J R R Tolkein, author of *Lord of the Rings*, said that it was seeing the coal trains, emblazoned with Welsh mine names, roll through his dreary suburb of Birmingham that awoke his interest in the Welsh language, and, from that, into inventing his own languages and worlds. Tolkein called Welsh 'the senior language of these islands', and many people, in Wales and beyond, have made the assumption that the ethereal gibberish of Elvish in his books (and the blockbuster movies that followed) was hugely influenced by Welsh. Mind you, there are plenty of acid-frazzled English émigrés in Wales who would swear blind that the *Lord of the Rings* was a documentary.

While eighteenth century visitors like Wordsworth, Coleridge, Turner, Defoe and Dr Johnson saw Wales in little more than purely physical terms, nineteenth-century travellers generally dug deeper for some understanding of the country, its history and its culture. The culture, in particular, became a bauble of endless fascination for some of the more romantic wayfarers, and numerous commentators remarked upon how well-read and literate working class Welsh people were. Poet Matthew Arnold, for example, addressed the 1866 National Eisteddfod, at Chester, with these words: 'When I see the enthusiasm these Eisteddfods can awaken in your whole people, and then think of the tastes, the literature, the amusements of our own lower and middle classes, I am filled with admiration.' That most romantic of all Saxon travellers, George Borrow, in *Wild Wales*, waxed even more lyrical, after holding a discussion about poetry (and the poet Huw Morris in particular) with a couple of Welsh millers: 'What a difference... between a Welshman and an Englishman of the lower class. What would a Suffolk miller's swain have said if I repeated to him verses out of Beowulf or even Chaucer...?'

Wild Wales, Borrow's account of his marathon 1854 ramble around the country, is the best example of the romantic

Englishman's take on Wales. Borrow had previously spent time in Spain and amongst British Romany gypsies, using his considerable talent for languages and his enthusiasm for knowledge to ingratiate himself with both peoples. He used the same technique for his trip to Wales, gaining a reasonable standard in spoken Welsh, in order to boom and bluster his way around the country. If the Romantic painters and Grand Tour playboys were Wales' first modern landscape tourists, then George Borrow spearheaded the arrival of the cultural tourist.

The WalesWorld Theme Park

It seems to be no coincidence that the Severn Bridge tolls only operate one way; namely, for westbound traffic coming into Wales. Cross either of the bridges into England and it will cost you nowt. Come the other way, into Wales, however, and it'll set you back a fiver. It only serves to reinforce the feeling that you are entering some kind of theme park, WalesWorld (*Where The Past Comes Alive!©*). You wouldn't blink if the toll booth attendant handed over a welcome leaflet, complete with information on to how to locate the Lost Children's Corner (Merthyr, probably) and which attractions are closed for essential maintenance (ditto).

Tourism is now the single biggest area of the Welsh economy, accounting for something over ten per cent of jobs. After scouring the country for five editions of the *Rough Guide to Wales*, what screamed to me as the single most obvious aspect of the country's tourist industry was just how much of it is owned and run by English rat race refugees. Estimates are that something over a half of Welsh hotels, B&Bs and pubs in tourist areas are run by people who hail from England. This is borne out by statistics and surveys, conducted on a regular basis, such as a highly detailed one produced for Aberystwyth University in 2001, that examined the population make-up in three areas of north-west Wales. In the area of Llanfair Mathafarn Eithaf, on Ynys Môn (Anglesey), which includes the popular resort of Benllech, it transpired that 81% of people working in tourism there were English incomers, and that three-quarters of those involved with tourism in this most Welsh-speaking of areas had no knowledge of the language. It is a deeply unhealthy, divisive situation.

Of course not all the blame for tourism's deficiencies should be laid at the door of the incomers. But taking into account the statistics quoted above, it is fair to argue that tourist operators who have settled here inevitably tilt their emphasis towards people like themselves, so that Wales is portrayed and marketed as nothing more than a big chill out zone away from urban (English) living. So much of the tourist industry's marketing plays to this tune, both individually, from hotels, B&Bs and attractions, and on a national scale, through organisations like the Wales Tourist Board. While it is true that a few days in rural or coastal Wales can be a sure-fire pick-me-up for someone used to a high-pressure city environment, to portray the country in such simplistic ways is little more than just a modern version of the mannered falseness of the Picturesque movement. It does nothing to portray the reality of modern Wales.

It does little, either, to deal with the historical and cultural complexity of the country. As poet Robert Minhinnick put it, in *A Postcard Home* (1994): 'Tourism is now the most important Welsh industry, and tourism is doing its level best to destroy what many people consider the two essential characteristics of Wales – its environment and its culture.' Welsh culture, where it appears in the marketing profile of so many companies, is reduced to a few misty Celtic clichés and, perhaps, a token smattering of Cymraeg or *y ddraig goch* (red dragon).

The blame, however, should not be wholly shouldered by those who move in and try to make a living out of offering a neatly-packaged holiday version of the aspects of Wales that first attracted them here. If people from London are willing to pay four hundred quid for a wet weekend in a tipi and a rub-down with patchouli oil from some local hippy, then more fool them and good luck to the people ripping off the daft saps. Far, far worse is the contribution of the taxpayer-funded agencies that, even in these days of supposed devolution, do nothing to attempt to remedy the highly skewed picture. Inter-Wales tourism, i.e. attracting visitors from one part of the country to another, is lamentably ignored. This is a potentially huge market: there are tens of thousands of people in, say, the Valleys, who have never been further north than Brecon, and similar numbers in Gwynedd, who have never visited their own capital city or, say, Pembrokeshire. The comment I get almost every day from Welsh people, in response to my TV travelogues around Wales, is how they have never visited many of the places featured in the programmes. When ITV Wales slashed their budgets, the production company I work with approached all manner of Welsh companies and organisations with a view to part-sponsoring my *Great Welsh Roads* series. One of the most telling responses came from one of the three regional Welsh tourist boards, who said that they had no interest in putting money into a series that was only shown within Wales. Were they to be shown in England, it would, they said, be a different matter.

This is short-sightedness in the extreme, but, sadly, not surprising. So entrenched is the idea in Welsh tourism that the visitors here come only from north-west England (to north Wales), the West Midlands (to mid Wales) and London (for south Wales), that these are the only areas that many tourism promoters ever bother with. If that's just about excusable from private companies, it's a disgrace when organisations funded entirely or partly from the public purse, from the National Assembly in particular, continue to act in such a tired, unimaginative way.

An emphasis on the traditional holiday markets, and its extension into the 'Chill out in Wales' branding, is also detrimental to the Welshness of the country. Put bluntly, many of the kind of tourists it is aimed at are the sort of people who feel faintly uneasy around the Welsh language, or any other kind of manifestations of real distinctiveness, this side of Offa's Dyke. They want the beauty of the landscape, but deracinated and packaged like a 3D postcard. Thus, southern Pembrokeshire, an area that has been known for the best part of a thousand years as Little England beyond Wales, is comprehensively anglicised and such a contrast with, say, the north of the county, or neighbouring Carmarthenshire. It is a safe haven for those who want a de-Welshified Wales – and there are many eager for that.

Even in the heartlands of Welsh culture and language, the tourism industry often goes out of its way to ignore the land that hosts it. In mid Wales, I recently went to an upmarket timeshare complex, grouped around an impressive eighteenth century Plas. All the lodges are given names designed to provoke in their guests feelings of hearty outdoor life. A signpost by the reception points them out: there's Windermere and Aviemore, Cairngorm and Ullswater. Not one is named after anywhere Welsh. And there's no other word of Welsh to be seen throughout the entire complex. It's designed for people who want to be surrounded by Wales, but stay deep within a little central bubble of Anglicised pretence. Mind you, all became clearer when I saw the health club's gym at this complex. Pride of place in the middle of the room is one of those walking machines, a conveyor belt you set to a chosen speed and walk on the spot for half an hour. Around all the walls are huge picture windows with gorgeous views over the surrounding mountains, so you can pound your way along a bit of vulcanised rubber while gazing at the magnificent peaks. Er, wouldn't it be better just to go for a bloody walk?

I don't get the (to quote *Twin Town*) Dinky Dooey Miniature Railway thing either. Wales is often held up as the unofficial capital of the Great Little Trains, but it's not something we should be cheering too loudly. Although I've enjoyed chugs on the Ffestiniog Railway as much as the next nerd, I am getting heartily sick of Wales' over-dependence on these toy trains as a staple of the tourist industry. It breaks my heart to see once proud communities, such as the Garw Valley, near Bridgend, reduced to searching for a new option for economic sustenance and managing only to come up with yet another steam railway (The Daffodil Line, Lord help us) as the answer. We have quite enough of them. But still they keep coming, and not – as they once were – just as voluntary schemes to keep train-spotters busy on a Sunday, but increasingly as full-scale, statutory projects, flagged up as the centre-piece for local regeneration.

We live in a country hampered terribly by its lack of integrated public transport, and yet the only railway-building projects happening in Wales at the moment are for these toy trains. Loads of the twenty existing steam railways in Wales are working hard to extend their length by a mile or so here, a couple of hundred yards there. In the bigger picture of Welsh public transport, they are, at best, an utter irrelevance, and, at worst, greedily soaking up valuable money that could be used to far better means.

To that end, although most of their finance comes from private and charity sources, many have also been on the receiving end of public money, either directly or indirectly, through Lottery funding, county council, National Assembly and Wales Tourist Board grants and European Union Objective One cash: Gwynedd's Rheilffordd Eryri (Welsh Highland Railway) alone has received over £10 million, and counting, from various sources. There are huge sums involved.

The most spurious reasoning given for this splurge of statutory support is that such schemes benefit the local population as much as tourists. Every single project blathers on cheerily about how preserved steam railways will be essential cogs in the wheel of local public transport. Quite how these can be seen as a useful commuting option is beyond me. They are expensive, monumentally slow and seasonal trains that don't even run for most of the year, and which – all too often – don't connect up with any other public transport at either end. Surely, a *real* railway might be more useful, to locals and tourists alike?

Taking a step back from the nitty-gritty of operating and funding these projects, there's plenty of cause for concern in their very foundation. Take a look at the websites of any of the Welsh steam railways, and nine out of ten of the grinning faces that you will see working on them belong to men over a certain age, the majority of them apparently weekending trippers from urban England. These blokes, for whom steam trains are a powerful nostalgia trip back to their own boyhoods, will, over the next couple of decades, be, quite literally, a dying breed. Where then for their oversized train sets? To be pouring time and money into projects with a likely built-in shelf life of no more than, say, twenty years is sadly typical of the lack of long-term thinking in economic development.

It's also typical of the rose-tinted nostalgia that infects far too much of the Welsh tourist industry, one that we are constantly reminded is the country's biggest single earner these days. Our hang-up on the so-called glory days of the industrial age has to be overcome if Wales is to develop into a country with a future, rather than just one with a heck of a past. Steam railways are one of the unhealthiest culprits of all, exacerbating, as they do, some kind of naff, folksy image of Wales as a land of little Tolkeinesque pixies, riding their miniature choo-choos to the coal mine or slate quarry. It's an image we should be stridently discouraging, not throwing money at. The *Sunday Times'* arch Cymrophobe, A A Gill, said of the Welsh landscape that, 'Everything that wasn't designed by God looks as if it was built by a hobbit.' For God's sake, we don't need to give him his ammunition on a plate!

Tourism in Wales is increasingly peddling this fantasy version of the country, and it's no surprise that many of the worst protagonists are people who have fled here in the first place because they can't cope with modern life back at home. Whether it's the 'Living Medieval', some dewy cod-Celtic nonsense, or the ubiquitous Industrial Heritage, there's the gnawing feeling that it's the past which matters most, and who cares how woolly or wildly inaccurate the interpretation of that past might be? In itself, the urge to glorify and romanticise the past, out of a deep-seated fear of the present, is an age-old phenomenon, and, over the years, it's brought a steady stream of English refugees to Wales. The Victorian vision of Wales depended much on a saccharine notion of the idealized harmony of 'cottage, throne and altar': George Borrow was its most enthusiastic subscriber. Touring Wales, he shunned the noisy, modern railways, shivered in horror at the animalistic colliers in the Valleys, and was happiest when what he saw most accurately chimed in with his memories of his own childhood. Today, we see precisely the same motivation in many rat race escapees: Wales as the imagined living embodiment of their own golden childhoods – a singularly unreliable and subjective memory, and one which is ultimately destined to remain tantalisingly out of reach.

When the tourism industry depends so much on re-packaging and re-selling this past, it can do real damage. It's a depressing thought, that regularly surfaces in my mind when I travel in the former industrial parts of Wales. Such was the speed of industry's arrival in, say, the Valleys, and such was the breakneck pace and viciousness of its destruction, that the shock has resulted in just about every rusty old remnant being clapped in the aspic of Heritage. And then we wonder why so many youngsters growing up in such areas go off the rails – well, all they see around them are signs of a noble, turbulent

Entrance to the Conwy Falls: Tourism Macht Frei.

past, but next to nothing that says anything hopeful or useful about the present or the future. Imagine growing up with that as the prevailing backdrop, and imagine what it would do for your self-esteem and sense of hope.

This would be a peripheral point, were the tourism industry not so all-conquering these days. In many parts of rural Wales (i.e. most of the country), it has become the sole industry. And now, other places, even those with very little tourism historically, are looking at the industry and thinking that, well, what the heck, we might as well go for it, as well. I recently spent a few days in Milford Haven. It's a town that has already seen three very different industries – whale oil, fishing and petrochemicals – rise and fall in its short history of just two centuries, each fall leaving the town a little more knackered than the last. Every time I asked anyone what they thought could replace the gradually disappearing refineries, their eyes glazed over, their shoulders shrugged and, with an air of torpid resignation, they'd say, 'Well, tourism, I suppose.' To that end, the town is full of glossy brochures exhorting the world to take Milford Haven seriously as a destination for cruise ships. Why go to the Bahamas, when you could cosy up alongside a Texaco tanker in gale-force winds? All too often, economically and culturally, tourism is not a position of strength, but an admission of defeat; the sole option of the damned.

Tourism is all well and good as part of a mixed economy, but when it becomes practically the only trade, it does few favours to its host community, providing largely seasonal, and often badly paid, jobs, and tending to skew the culture of an area towards a bland parody of itself, just for the sake of the visitors. Parts of Ireland, which have become utterly prostituted to the tourist dollar and a pale imitation of their former selves as a result, are a sharp wake-up call for us here in Wales.

This is perhaps the central issue in relation to Welsh tourism: just how Welsh is it allowed to be? It's inescapably true that, amongst tourism operators in Wales, a far higher proportion are incomers, usually English, than in the population at large. While some do their utmost to be sensitive to local culture, all too often it is airbrushed out of the picture, or given just token recognition (the odd bilingual sign, a flag, or use of a Celtic typeface, if they're feeling particularly generous). In his *Notes from a Small Island*, Bill Bryson muses on the subject of Llandudno B&Bs:

> *Almost without exception they had names that bore homage to other places – Windermere, Stratford, Clovelly, Derby, St Kilda, even Toronto – as if their owners feared that it would be too much of a shock to the system to remind visitors that they were in Wales. Only one place, with a sign that said Gwely a Brecwast/Bed and Breakfast, gave any hint that I was, at least in a technical sense, abroad.*

As the recent controversies over the developments at Pwllheli marina and the Bluestone project in Pembrokeshire have demonstrated, tourism decisions can have a huge and retrogressive impact on local culture, already fragile enough in many parts of rural Wales. Now that tourism is the single biggest industry in Wales, serious questions need to be addressed as to exactly how much and what kind we need in the future. However much tourism operators are encouraged to flag up the illusion of Welshness in their operation, or make overblown claims for how many jobs their project will bring to an area, history and the evidence in front of our noses shows that the jobs rarely materialise quite as promised and, more importantly perhaps, that unbridled tourism inevitably brings unbridled Anglicisation with it, and turns a place into yet another washed-out pastiche of itself. Sometimes, it means we

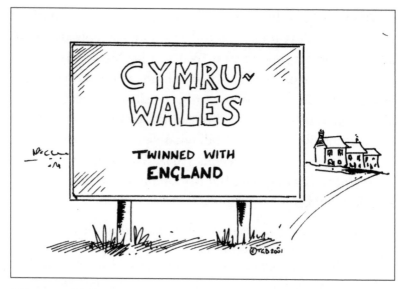

Original cartoon: Toby Driver

have to say no to further development; a short-term denial for long-term gain.

The Fat of the Land

The past forty years have seen a massive influx of English Good Lifers into most corners of rural Wales. Many have truly integrated into their local communities, showing sensitivity to the fragility of the language and culture in their new homes. Often, those with young children enmesh themselves more easily into their host locale, as chats at the school gate, PTA meetings, fetes, parties and so on are very good ways of gelling with your neighbours. A fair few incomers sign up to Welsh classes – and some even stick at them (but, sadly, not many. It is a grim statistic that only five percent of people – one in twenty – who start learning Welsh see it through to any degree of competent fluency). Some become fascinated by aspects of

Welsh history and culture and immerse themselves in learning more about the land that they now call home. But for every keen Welsh learner or sympathetic *Cymro manqué* (as I was once memorably called), there are many more who barely bother to engage at all with their host culture. Indeed, the Good Lifers – the Jeremys and Jemimas who want to knit their own yoghurt and not hurt a fly – are often the worst culprits.

In the area of mid Wales where I live, the largest employer is the Centre for Alternative Technology (CAT), which has sat up in its old slate quarry near Machynlleth for over thirty years now. CAT is one of the best examples of something set up by

"The Dyfi valley is backing no war." Painted on a wind turbine above Machynlleth. That'll tell 'em.

Photo: author

liberal English incomers, which has now folded its way into the life and landscape of its area. There are many wonderful people involved with the place, who care passionately about the world and what is going on within it. But, still, patronising and paternalistic thoughtlessness creeps in. To the outside world, CAT and green businesses like it are shining examples of creating a new way of living. To many local people, there is a sense of something rather darker, and more oppressive, lurking in all the rosy-cheeked, back-to-the-land heartiness.

For starters, despite having been there for over three decades now, CAT has virtually no Welsh members of staff, and none at all in anything like a senior position. Just like the mine and quarry owners of a century before, the local workforce has been used as a source for only the menial or low-ranking jobs, while all the managers and top brass have come from elsewhere. When approached by S4C for input into a change-your-life series, CAT could find only one Welsh speaker to go on the programme (and him in their shop in Machynlleth town centre) from amongst their roster of over eighty paid employees. In earlier times, a Welsh-speaking employee in CAT's café in Machynlleth was harshly told off for daring to speak the language in front of customers, an old chestnut that we normally associate with ruthless supermarket chains rather than a vegetarian café run by hippies.

It is, however, the more nebulous aspects of New Age condescension that tell us more than the odd outbreak of crass cultural insensitivity. Many of the local people that I have spoken to over the last few years have confessed to a sense of deep unease at the attitudes they have encountered from the hundreds of brightly-jumpered *Guardian* devotees attracted to the area by CAT and its cohorts. I've seen and heard it plenty of times myself, too: throwaway remarks or crashing assumptions that reveal, beneath all the internationalist bluster, a disconcerting arrogance towards (and ignorance of) Welsh culture. Never underestimate the zeal of the convert; especially if that convert hails from a culture I know all too well, namely middle-class Middle England. They arrive in rural, Welsh-speaking Wales, fired up with a righteous sense of 'doing the right thing' in their environmental work, and nothing is allowed to dent that.

Underpinning many of these attitudes is a deep-rooted certainty on behalf of the incomers that they have far more to teach the Welsh than the other way round. They truly believe that they are bringing into the relationship with their new locale the lion's share of valuable qualities: sophistication, liberal cosmopolitanism, 'progress', a breath (as they see it) of much-needed fresh air. By implication, such assumptions rubbish the qualities of the indigenous culture, its spirited survival, its longevity, its rootedness, its emphasis on community over rampant individualism, its creativity and huge sense of fun, its spirituality, its less strident, but very present, nonetheless, pluralism and tolerance. All too rarely do the more arrogant incomers stay quiet long enough to hear such delicate (and increasingly fragile) qualities breathe. At best, this is supremely patronising. At worst, it's downright hostile.

Worse is when such incomers start to believe their own hype, and start to make strident claims that it is their presence that has 'saved' rural Wales. All too many truly believe it. During the devolution referendum, the *New York Times* published quite an in-depth report on the campaign, and Wales' status as a whole, digging up a stalwart of the Just Say No campaign in Llanwrtyd Wells, an English woman who had moved there. She was quoted as saying that she was opposed to the Assembly, for, 'My concern is for towns like this, towns that have been kept alive by the English who come here to live and who support local institutions.' The article continued: 'She argued that the costs of the new bureaucracy would be passed down to individuals and would end up driving more Welsh out of the country and removing the economic advantages that bring people of means to Wales.' People of means. People like us. We are the ones that matter.

Even on their home ground topic of environmentalism, many of the incomers seem to believe that they are bringing something bright and light into the poor, dark little worlds of local people, something that they couldn't possibly begin to understand, unless a kindly environmentalist is there to explain it for them. Community-funded wind turbines and biomass furnaces are routinely presented to every local village as the answer to their prayers, and any doubt or opposition is firmly squashed by cunning use of the English middle-class's innate ability to bulldoze, in the nicest possible way, their ideas through others' lack of confidence. Ironically, green energy is an area that local people need no introduction to. For most of the villages in the area, their first taste of electricity came through community-based hydro-electric schemes running from fast-flowing rivers. These successfully sustained many villages for decades, without anyone in a multi-coloured jumper telling them how to do it.

One of the earliest pioneers – and that's really how they saw themselves – of self-sustaining English incomers into Wales was the author John Seymour (1914 – 2004). He and his then wife, Sally, moved to a smallholding on the slopes of the Mynydd Preseli, in Pembrokeshire, in 1965, which quickly became a beacon to those who were growing increasingly turned-off by the technology of the twentieth century. Seymour's books, including *The Complete Guide to Self-Sufficiency*, *Fat of the Land* and *I'm A Stranger Here Myself*, sold by the shed load in the oil-worried 1970s. He was, for sure, an inspirational character, even if he was apparently, by the admission of many friends and family, something of a drunkard, a bit of a bully and a womaniser. After his death, his daughter Ann said of her father, 'He had a lot of wives and children. He treated them all badly and loved them.'

Seymour's is a pattern that seems fairly common in many of the self-appointed English 'leaders' of green living in Wales: they are almost always men of quite (or very) posh backgrounds, and invariably described as 'larger than life'. This is frequently a euphemism for a congenital piss-artist, who shags his way through every wide-eyed young hippy girl, eager for inspiration, who tripped up to the door. I have come across so many men like this, blokes who like to believe that they are finding exciting, revolutionary new ways of living, but who, in their personal lives, are acting with all of the finesse of unreconstructed shag-monsters, the very sort of men to whom they loftily believe themselves to be vastly superior. Masking their lechery behind a gauze veil of touchy-feely New Agery, combined with copious quantities of drink and drugs and helped by the lacerating self-doubt of their victims, they cut their self-indulgent swathe through as many young women as they can. If the personal is political, their politics stink.

Even the B-team of New Age men often come laden with sexual politics that are laughable in their puerility. Some of the most immature, and deeply-rooted, homophobia I've ever experienced has come from men like this – way, way worse, I might add, than anything I've ever heard in a Welsh rugby club, or working men's institute. Not long ago, I watched with incredulity as a young hippy couple, a riot of tie-dye and dreadlocks, made their way down the street of a west Wales market town. The girl, a good ten yards behind the man, was struggling under the weight of a large baby and three or four bags of shopping. The lad, bouncing along contentedly on the balls of his feet, way up ahead, was carrying only his precious didgeridoo, slung nonchalantly over his shoulder. Change their outfits, and you could have been looking at a shell-suited couple in any English inner city. Peace and love, man.

Chapter 6

CRYSTAL BALLS:
Where Next?

*'To me,' said the poet and novelist Glyn Jones, 'anyone can be
a Welshman who chooses to be so, and is prepared to take the
consequences.' Gwyn Alfred Williams, the remembrancer of the
people of Wales as he has been called, made much the same
point in typical fashion: 'If we want Wales, we will have to
make Wales.'*

Prof R R Davies, address to Cymmorodion Society, May 2002

So what of the future of this ancient relationship? Can the
English and the Welsh ever learn truly to love each other,
instead of staring warily over the leylandii? And, if that is to
happen, what must take place before it can come into being?

Most importantly, I believe that the English need to deal
with their post-colonial hang-ups. It seems increasingly true
that so much of the antagonism and bile that I've catalogued
in these pages stems from a strange sense of English unease
about their nearest, and oldest, neighbours. As Richard Jones
put it, in *The New Welsh Review*, in 1992:

> *This English need to play down and despise all things Welsh
> appears to come from some deep complex that is beyond the
> reach of reason. Do they feel some ancient resentment that they
> were not the first people on this island, or do they simply resent
> a group that does not accept automatically everything they
> stand for?*

Having spent many years immersed in both sides of the

The joys of Britishness. Abertillery, June 2006.
Photo: author

argument, I can only conclude that the answer to his question is yes. In this technological day and age, we're not much encouraged to think about the insubstantialities of life that hang unquantifiably in the ether, but it is there that I think we find some ancient collective memory, a resentment, that underpins it all. The very fact that the same old put-downs seem to have travelled through the centuries, unchecked and unchanged, suggests that we are dealing here with antique forces. Maybe we will never get over them, but I don't believe that that should stop us from trying. Both nations would have much to gain if we did.

Baywatch

The partial devolution afforded to the National Assembly in Cardiff Bay has, to date, been a fairly effective way of lancing the boil of modern Welsh nationalism, one that had been rising steadily through the Thatcher and Major years of the eighties and nineties. Few people could have justified the situation under the last Conservative government, where one Secretary of State for Wales – the last four Tory incumbents all being English MPs from English constituencies – held quite so many purse-strings at once. Wales was fast becoming known as a quangocracy, a fiefdom run by a small handful of unelected political yes-men. Even the most anti-Welsh nationalist had reluctantly to admit that the much-vaunted democratic deficit in Wales was yawning wide and growing by the day.

When Tony Blair came to power in 1997, the Labour party were largely committed to partial devolution for Scotland and Wales, albeit different amounts for the two countries. As can be seen in the entire history of the relationship between the Labour Party and Wales, the policy agreed on was something of a fudge, in order to keep on board both the devolution-sceptics and enthusiasts within the party's ranks. Labour has always had a slightly strained approach to its own Welshness, and there have always been plenty of Labour MPs (and now AMs) whose main political skill is sniffing out and stridently denouncing any hint of pro-Welsh bias in anything, from the contents of their own manifestoes to the corridors of, say, the Arts Council or the BBC. Thus it was with the devolution proposals. Originally, when John Smith was still alive and leader of the Labour Party, the scheme was to have been automatically rolled out, on the election of a Labour government. The diehard sceptics in Labour's own ranks ensured that this was changed, and that devolution would only go ahead subject to a referendum.

Of course, this being Wales, the devolution referendum vote went down to the wire. It was only when the very final vote came in from Carmarthenshire that the balance tipped back to a Yes vote, and then by the most wafer-thin of majorities. Since then, those who fundamentally disagree with the idea of any kind of all-Wales forum have used any and every occasion to remind us of the closeness of this vote. Thankfully, though, their numbers are gradually diminishing, but there remains a hardcore of sceptics in Wales – many of them vocal, English in-migrants – who loathe the Assembly simply for being there, and waste no chance to rubbish and belittle it. They are the ones who write letters to local papers throughout Wales, every week, bewailing anything the Assembly does, and using any perceived weakness, or run-of-the-mill political scandal in the institution to call into question its very right to exist.

As I write, the latest such moan centres on the Assembly's new Cardiff Bay building, opened in February 2006. In my local weekly paper (the *Cambrian News*), there is a typical letter from a representative of the UK Independence Party (UKIP), who states disingenuously, 'Just think of the number of NHS dentists £67 million [the cost of the new Senedd] would pay for.' I think we can be safely confident that the UK government in London has wasted £67 million, over and over again, on any number of projects (government PR, dubious consultancies, faulty computer systems, PFI scandals, illegal war and so on), but such things do not seem to bother UKIP and their ilk. This is the party, after all, that once fought an election on the manifesto promise: 'We will cut crime to the level of the 1950s' – a statement so simplistic it makes John Prescott sound like a political philosopher of Platonic proportions. Thinking that it's still 1955 seems to be the mainstay of most of their political outlook.

UKIP-thinking – by which I mean a *Daily Mail*-reading,

Little Englander conservatism – is a huge political force amongst many of the English in Wales. I have to confess that it fascinates me, for these people are often to be found in some of the most Welsh parts of Wales. Do they not see the irony? I once interviewed a former UKIP parliamentary candidate on one of my ITV Wales travelogue programmes. The interview wasn't about that, as such, but I recognised his name and face from party leaflets that had been pushed through my door. He is an old-school Tory, really, as are most in their ranks, and what particularly intrigued me was how we both saw the same area of land in such different ways. He looks at a map and the borders that sing to him are the old pre-1974 county boundaries (and nicely anglicised names) and the sea around the island of Great Britain. To him, that immortal *Times* headline, 'Fog in Channel: Continent Cut Off' is no joke, it's a statement of true perspective. I can look at exactly the same map, and it's the Welsh-English border that seems most interesting, followed by our contextual place in the continent of Europe. That said, I am quite fond of the old counties too – the counties of Rhondda-Cynon-Taff or Neath-Port Talbot could never inspire loyalty in anyone, except perhaps the worst kind of municipal paper-pusher.

With nearly a decade of partial devolution under our belts, there is a definite feeling of change in Welsh society. The National Assembly's difficult infant years have sadly coincided with a huge upsurge across the West of apathy towards all political establishments, and the Assembly, as the newest kid on the block, has reaped more than its fair share of that particular backdraught. Add to that the uniquely deep levels of venom aimed at the Assembly by those inconsolably hostile to its very existence and it's all too easy to get lost in the cynicism of the whole thing. Matters are hardly helped when Wales' self-declared National Newspaper, the *Western Mail*, doesn't even bother to keep a correspondent at the Assembly any more, and prefers to print only the more sensationalist stories that show it and its members in a decidedly dodgy light.

Go and take a look at the National Assembly, sit in on a debate or a committee. It's a long way from perfect, but there's something very important happening down there. Welsh issues are getting seriously examined in a Welsh context, a new civic society is being nurtured and a whole political and social infrastructure created across the nation. Those, including the many Labour MPs, who crave the Assembly's demise, want to turn their backs on all that and tie us firmly in with Westminster, somewhere that has never really understood or empathised with Wales, as our sole source of government. We should have the confidence to say that those days are gone, and head for the next stage in what was always promised to be 'a process, not an event'.

If the Welsh press' reporting from the National Assembly is sadly lacking, the response of the UK-wide London papers has been indifferent. Few stories from Cardiff Bay ever make it into their pages, and those that do are often couched in distinctly sniffy tones. To date, there have been only two occasions when the Westminster rat pack deigned to cover events in Cardiff to any definitive extent: firstly, when Alun Michael was voted out of office in early 2001, and, later the same year, when Tony Blair came to address the Assembly and used the occasion to make a much-vaunted defence of his plans in the so-called War on Terror, just seven weeks after the 9/11 attacks in New York and Washington. For once, London political journalists winkled themselves out of the febrile atmosphere of the Palace of Westminster and clambered aboard the Cardiff train, to take a look at the new institution. Their response was predictably haughty: despite the meat of the matter being discussed, the sketch-writers all managed a few sideswipes at the unglamorous surroundings of the National Assembly.

To Matthew Parris, in *The Times*, the debating chamber reminded him of a bar on a 1980s cross-channel ferry. Simon Hoggart, in *The Guardian*, stretched a similar analogy further:

> What a pity then that [Blair's big speech] had to be delivered at the Welsh assembly, whose chamber resembles a function room in a provincial hotel. You can see the ads: For your next conference or presentation, why not try our Assembly Suite? This luxurious room can be tailored to your individual needs, and a wide range of refreshments can be served.

So far, so mildly amusing. *The Daily Telegraph*'s resident sketch-writer (Frank Johnson) though, true to his distinctly second-rate musings, conflated the whole War on Terror speech with his observations on Wales, and kept pumping until it popped, in a big gooey journalistic mess:

> The Prime Minister yesterday shouted defiance of Osama bin Laden from a hideout somewhere in Wales. Al-Qa'eda's intelligence analysts were probably able roughly to locate the part of that wild, mountainous country where he was speaking: the newly-devolved Welsh Assembly. They would have done so by identifying the dense, grey geological formations surrounding him: some of the members of the newly devolved Welsh Assembly. This does not mean that Al-Qa'eda is any nearer finding Mr Blair. Now they must face the possibility that Wales has joined the international coalition against them.
>
> Mr bin Laden would have been warned that a Welsh force could be on its way to Afghanistan, possibly the Welsh Guards, perhaps the Welsh rugby team, which has long fancied its chances in a game against the Al Qa'eda XV.

It could have been worse from Mr bin Laden's point of view. It could have been one of Wales's feared male voice choirs. True, they sometimes hit civilian ear drums. But, when they go into action, some collateral damage is unavoidable. This is no time for liberal scruples.

Even with an Assembly, however, there are telling signs that the old colonialism just won't lie down. When the former President of Plaid Cymru, Dafydd Wigley, questioned Tony Blair in the House of Commons about the limited powers of the new body, Blair reverted to type and let out a petty little sideswipe that said perhaps more than he intended: 'We give him an assembly in Wales, and he still complains... It would be good once in a while to get a bit of gratitude.' It was that old stance again, that of an exasperated parent with a grumpy child. It surprised no-one particularly when ex-Downing Street press officer, Lance Price, published his diaries in 2005, and revealed the British Prime Minister's reaction to the first Welsh Assembly elections of May 1999, when the Labour party did so badly. Price claimed that Blair repeatedly exclaimed, 'The fucking Welsh!' in fury as the results rolled in. Had he been reported as saying that about any other racial or ethnic grouping in Britain, it's hard to imagine that he would have survived until the next morning. Small wonder that an African journalist, sent over to Cardiff to report on the 1997 devolution referendum, stated sadly, 'The colonial mentality is more firmly entrenched in your country than in any other I have been to.'

Wales with a Waitrose

Outside of the machinations of party and electoral politics, there are many other more pressing matters determining the future of the relationship between England and Wales, and the English in Wales in particular. Without question, the thorniest is that of house prices. Is there no end to the brain-shrivelling insanity around the issue? Until recently, Wales was fortunate to be out of the frame as far as ridiculous, spiralling house values went. Sadly, it is no more. The mania has filtered out, like ripples on a pond, from the south-east of England, where it originated in the get-rich-quick 1980s. Nowhere is now immune.

In certain sections of the Welsh press, this madness is presented as twenty-four carat good news. To their warped way of thinking, it gives new cachet to Wales. Excited *Daily Post* and *Western Mail* headlines boast that Gwynedd house prices boomed by 57 per cent in 2003 alone, or that Wales is now stuffed with £1 million plus houses. But it is not good news. A few people (the usual suspects: estate agents, developers,

Wales, the new Cornwall. Property, the new heroin.
Photo: author

solicitors and banks) are the winners, but the vast majority of us lose out. Aside from the ever higher mortgages that they are striving hard to serve, anyone who already owns a house might be better off on paper, but, should they want to sell up and move, prices everywhere else will be similarly inflated. There's no free money; it's all relative. Then, there are the tens of thousands of youngsters and local first-time buyers for whom the bottom rung of the property ladder is fast disappearing from view.

The Welsh property market is in a uniquely perilous state, and urgent action is required. The pressures on it are immense. Firstly, there are increasing numbers of speculators, who have decided that, with global capitalism looking decidedly rickety, there's little point in stashing your cash in anything that's not solid – and there's nothing so solid as property. To compound the covetous urges, Gordon Brown's Budget tax breaks made it even easier for people to buy second, or even third, houses, although late rule changes have, thankfully, tamed some of the worst excesses of this. But still, Wales, with its, until recently, relatively low house prices, combined with our tremendous natural landscape, has proved to be fertile ground for the speculative, the acquisitive and the just plain greedy.

To make Wales more appealing to middle-class, English, relocation TV show addicts, it needs to be de-Welshified, and that is a process going on apace. Lavish features in broadsheet property sections declare Monmouthshire to be 'the new Cotswolds', or even, when they're feeling particularly giddy, 'the new Tuscany'. One such piece, in the *Sunday Times*, was titled 'Wales with a Waitrose', thus hitting the g-spot for twitchy Londoners stoked up with the half-a-million quid they anticipate getting for their four-bedroom semis. In the piece, a Cardiff-based property expert, specialising in south-east Wales, declared that, 'A psychological barrier has been broken. People are now crossing the River Severn and are prepared to say they live in Wales.' Well, bully for them. The article also points out that 90 per cent of those who voted in the area opposed the creation of the Welsh Assembly. The message is clear. It might be Wales, but it's OK. It's not too Welsh, and you're very unlikely to be harangued by nasty nationalists, or have little Octavia forced into learning that beastly Cymraeg. You can just go to Waitrose, and pretend you're in Cheltenham.

Similar pieces have been appearing in the London broadsheet property sections at increasingly regular intervals. A *Daily Telegraph* piece in July 2005 included a lengthy feature on a mid Wales property that was going for a cool half-million quid. There was the usual guff about an unpronounceable name, which, 'like so much in Welsh, sounds like a murderous threat uttered by a man preparing to spit', and the piece quoted the Londoner owner as saying, 'It will probably be bought by people like us – people looking for a change of life, who want a slow-paced environment?' The thought that anyone local might be interested obviously hadn't even entered his little head. But, at £500,000, he's probably right. At the end of October 2004, *The Sunday Telegraph* devoted two pages to a huge piece ('The Brecons Beckon', ugh!), which had as its sub-head the following toe-curling crap: 'With the Cotswolds too costly, Wales has become the new frontier for urban émigrés. Emily Bearn is pleasantly surprised to find a welcome – and a Waitrose – in the hillsides.' (That bloody Waitrose again!) Highlighted out of the article was a quotation from a Hereford estate agent: 'People have got over that 'Oh dear, it's Wales' feeling... they realise it is easy to get to.' And, it's to be hoped, easy to get away from too, preferably for good.

It's a fairly cast iron rule-of-thumb, that if a Welsh property is placed on the market in the hands of an English estate agent (usually in Hereford, Cheltenham, Chester, Shrewsbury or Bristol), the vendors are hoping for a wealthy, middle-class English buyer, preferably someone downshifting from London. While this can be mildly irritating for the owners of Welsh properties in the borders, it becomes something a whole load more sinister when the houses in question are deep in Welsh Wales, be it the west, north or middle of the country. Perhaps the most startling example to date came in 2003, when the owner of one of the most westerly houses in Wales, overlooking Ynys Dewi, Ramsey Island, in Pembrokeshire, placed his house on the market with an upmarket agent in Tetbury, Gloucestershire, for a sneeze under £1 million. In an advert for the house, in *The Daily Telegraph*, it was baldly stated that, 'The vendors are hoping to sell to a holiday home owner, rather than a local.' Hardly surprisingly, this caused huge offence locally – and you can only presume that that was precisely what the vendor intended. It becomes even more distasteful when you realise that the sale included the ruins of St Justinian's chapel, a hugely important relic of the great Welsh Age of the Saints, on the prissily-cut lawns of the house.

While insisting that only gentrified English estate agents should sell your Welsh property is cheesy enough, it should certainly not be inferred that all is going to be just fine and dandy if you go through an estate agent in Wales. It is noticeable how different agencies specialise in different kinds of property, aimed at very different markets. There are old-fashioned, locally-based agents, many specialising in family farms, agricultural auctions and the less glamorous house sales. Just down the street will be the swish offices of some newer agents, staffed by people with no hint of a Welsh accent, who go out of their way to make the whole experience as unthreatening, and English, as possible to the wallet-stuffed urban escapees who make up the vast majority of their client base. They sell a dream, one which very often fails to live up to its billing – which, for the estate agents, is just fine. After all, if the new owners give up after their second Welsh winter and flee back to Surrey, the chances are they'll get the opportunity to re-sell the same house, at an even bigger price, to the next batch of innocents. None of these kinds of agents give prospective buyers any information about just how different Wales is – culturally, historically, politically, socially – from suburban England. This is an even more glaring omission in areas like Anglesey, Gwynedd or Ceredigion, where Welsh is the majority language. But our politicians must shoulder some responsibility, too. A seismic shift is occurring, and occurring very quickly. If they don't take action to help redress the balance in favour of people wanting to stay in their own communities, it will shortly be too late.

When I was house-hunting, through 2000 and 2001 (I saw about seventy properties, scattered across mid Wales, in that time), it became very clear very quickly just how segregated the area has become. There are some villages that, in just thirty or so years, have become almost entirely populated by incomers, while other settlements, often just a mile or so up the road, remain pretty much wholly populated by local people. With all too many of the houses that I was seeing, I'd arrive, to be met by the English vendors, who, once they'd established that I, too, hailed from England, would go out of their way to assure me that the Welsh round here were either: a) none too numerous or b) easily patronised and/or ignored. There's a time-bomb slowly ticking in the hills.

Changing Perspective

> *Suddenly England, bourgeois England, wasn't my point of*
> *reference any more. I was a Welsh European [and] I want the*
> *Welsh people – still a radical and cultured people – to defeat,*
> *over-ride or by-pass bourgeois England.*

Raymond Williams, *Politics and Letters*, 1979

I'm not trying to pretend that mine is a model for how to be an Englishman in twenty-first century Wales. When I first moved here, after years of admiring it, idolising even, from afar, and then years spent writing about it for the *Rough Guide*, I was painfully guilty of trying too hard. I cringe to admit it now, but in my second month of being a citizen of Cymru, I was on the Wlpan intensive Welsh course at Aberystwyth University, and our tutor asked us all to write down, in English, our reasons for being there. In my rather pompous keenness, I recall writing something along the lines of: 'I want to be part of the Cymry Cymraeg, not an incomer.' Six years later, I realise all too well the hopeless naïveté of such a statement. I may well be in Wales for the rest of my life, but I will always be an incomer and, no matter how good my Welsh gets, how enthusiastically I write and broadcast about the country, or how many eisteddfodau I drag myself along to, I won't ever make it into the ranks of the Cymry Cymraeg. To aspire to that is to deny both history (Wales' *and* mine) and reality.

Another facet of life that I had entirely under-estimated in moving to Wales was the change in my perception of the landscape and all that is in it. When I was only ever coming to Wales as either a tourist, or a fired-up travel writer, it was easy to see only the intoxicating sweep of the Welsh landscape in an almost purely aesthetic way. Although I was reading everything I could lay my hands on about the history and heritage of the country, it tended towards a similarly romanticised outlook, and just added fuel to the flames of my misty passions. Actually living in that landscape, or rather, perhaps, *on* that landscape, changed everything utterly. Gradually, the real, backbreaking grind of the Welsh past and present, its pride and powerlessness, began to infuse every view and vista. Everywhere I looked, where I had once just seen a luscious visual feast, I now saw seams of painful social and cultural upheaval plaited into it. This is classic with any marginalised culture, for the signs don't necessarily reveal themselves on first inspection; but they are there, and to ignore them is like a child putting its fingers in its ears and shrilling 'la, la, la!' to avoid hearing something nasty. Sometimes, in my more downbeat moments, I wish for the impossible: that I could unlearn all of this and return to the days when I was able to see Wales only as a dazzling orgy of colour and form, devoid of content or context. Too late. Much, much too late. Yet again, that old curmudgeon, R S Thomas put it most succinctly:

> *To live in Wales is to be conscious*
> *At dusk of the spilled blood*
> *That went to the making of the wild sky*
>
> A Welsh Landscape

Being in rural Wales has completely changed the way I see the world, but, more importantly, it's changed the way I want to communicate that. Living and writing in a cynical, urban, English environment, with its million layers of smartarse one-upmanship, inevitably produced a cynical, world-weary take on life from me. It's the prevailing mindset; all very post-modern, post-ironic and post-bloody everything. In both my writing and stand-up, that cynicism infused everything. I could churn out pointed, acerbic little *bons mots* to editors and comedy club owners. I could snap my fingers, and pout, pose or fume on cue. Even when let out of my cage and packed off to Wales for the early editions of the *Rough Guide*, I was still framing my experiences through the prism of being clever-clever, and was, in truth, just as interested in finding pithy ways to put things down, as in attempting to understand or contextualise them.

It's the yawning gap between *Rough Guide* Wales and the real Wales that has most dramatically underlined the change to me. Like so much of the tourism industry that they support, guide books promote a reductive, bite-sized experience of the patch that they cover. Everything and everywhere is boiled down to its most basic ingredients. Anything too difficult or real is filtered out, in favour of the bland, the packaged and the unthreatening. In the thirteen years that I've been writing the *Rough Guide to Wales*, I've had countless arguments with editors, who complain that the book is too political, that I'd gone too native, and who then used that to expunge from my text its spikier content.

Even if they were prepared to let me say exactly what I wanted about places, I couldn't write the *Rough Guide* again. Like all guide books, especially those in large, international series, it has become deeply formulaic and inherently conservative in its scope and ambition. The Wales it portrays – of sweet little steam trains and *Guardian*-readers' gastro-pubs – is one that I surely recognise, but it's not one that interests me greatly any more. Of far greater appeal is the land that I see around me every day, a place of shit and sunshine, *hwyl* and heartbreak, often all at the same time.

When an EU statistical yearbook came out in 2004, with Wales inexplicably shorn off the map of Britain, Jan Morris wrote a cheerful response in *The Independent* to the extent that Wales was something of a country of the mind, anyway, so it mattered little whether it appeared on the maps churned out by officialdom. She made some deadly serious points amidst the banter, though; stating at one point that there are people in the Welshest part of Wales who are made so profoundly unhappy by the whittling away of their language, their values and their way of life that they are driven to alcoholism, driven to nervous breakdown. This statement brought a typically bullish response from Janet Street-Porter, in her column in its sister paper, the *Independent on Sunday*. Blaming the English for their love of the bottle? Street-Porter could hardly contain her glee as she laid into Morris' thinking, and it gave her yet another chance to have a pop at Wales. But Jan Morris had a perfectly valid point. Our cultural background – the one in which we're drenched from the earliest moment – dictates so much of our personal development. If you are born and raised in a culture that feels marginalised, threatened and necessarily defensive, that fact will seep into the way you see and experience everything. Incidences of, for instance, alcoholism can be seen in marginalised cultures the world over. Just to rubbish an idea or to wish that it were not so, does not make it untrue.

I stated in the preface to this book that, as I have been writing it, a hazy image of my ideal readers has swum into view; namely, my fellow in-migrants from England into Wales. This is very much for them: a call to change their horizons now that they are in a different country. It doesn't matter if their cultural diet is high or lowbrow, whether they are devotees of *The Guardian*, Radio 4 and the Discovery Channel, or *The Sun*, Radio 1 and Men & Motors. For many people, the fact that they can get the same newspapers, magazines, TV and radio that they previously had in England is reason enough not to bother changing lifelong habits, but, to make any success of life here, they really should. Keep to the old habits, sure, but augment them with some new ones.

Watch Welsh television, in both English and Welsh. Yes,

there is a lot of absolute shit on the box, but the Welsh channels have neither more nor less of it than any other channel. Tune into Radio Wales, Radio Cymru or local radio stations, to get used to the sound of Welsh and its many accents. Try reading *The Western Mail* every so often, or, as is to be fervently hoped, one of its much-anticipated new rivals, or one of the many superb periodicals that can be found in any Welsh shop or decent bookshop. Borrow some Welsh-published books from your local library. Go to classes in local and Welsh history, or to learn the language. Try concerts, gigs, festivals and theatre trips that you'd normally ignore, or decide that they're not for you. OK, a drama in Welsh, if your knowledge of Cymraeg isn't up to it, can be a mighty long, and frustrating, evening, but *gigs*? Why on earth do most Welsh-language bands, DJs and singers end up playing only to native Welsh speakers? This is music, for crying out loud, a whole language of its own. Jump in. Try it out. Be prepared to be surprised.

Living in Wales for six years now has sharpened my sense of my own Englishness. It's also made me respect and love it more. There are so many aspects of Englishness of which I'm wholly, heartily proud, from rolling hills to real ale, the Bard to the Beatles to Bhangra. The English might well be world-beaters in inventing anything that's buttoned-up and buffoonish, but they almost always, inadvertently, invent the exact opposite as well. At every turn in English history, repression begat A-grade rebellion: the Levellers and the Lollards; the Tolpuddle Martyrs; the Peasants' Revolt; the anti-slavery movement; those who halted Oswald Mosley at Cable Street, in London's East End; the Jarrow marchers and the Suffragettes, together with the countless writers and artists who sustained them. It's no coincidence, that from the same suburban discontent were born both Thatcherism, that zenith of petty, prodding Englishness, and gobbing, snarling punk, its exact antithesis. If there's one thing about which the English could learn much from their western cousins, it's a comfortable pride in themselves, that does not have to regress into a cartoon, curtain-twitching *Daily Mail*ism.

Yma o Hyd (Still here)

Much has been written and spoken in the last forty years of the effect of English in-migration into Wales. Like the regular prophecies of the imminent demise of the Welsh language that have surfaced with clockwork dependability throughout the last century, rarely does a year go by without invocation of the Doomsday scenario, where rural Wales has been strangled by wave upon wave of rat-race escapees. The first siren warnings were sounded in the 1960s, gathered pace through the seventies and eighties, and have, since the turn of the new millennium, reached some sort of shrill fever pitch.

Yet rural Wales still survives, flamboyantly and un-ambiguously Welsh in flavour and culture. Many of the most niggardly English incomers last only a year or two, before skulking back across the border, muttering darkly to themselves. Those who stay and thrive are, generally speaking, those who make some kind of effort to integrate and become part of the local fabric. In these days of such ready mobility, where any of us can – and do – move countries, continents even, with the minimum of fuss, there is something to be said for different places attracting those most suited to the local ambience, those most likely to give it their best shot. After all, if it doesn't work out, there's always somewhere else to try.

Consider these words from a book published thirty years ago, spoken by a woman who had moved from England into Carmarthenshire. 'We'll admit that it is harder than we imagined, but all the more rewarding for that. We have learned to speak Welsh and our three children are bi-lingual. We believe that immigrants should go more than half-way to meet local people and become a part of the local scene. It is important to contribute to local life and defend it and not stand outside it.' Every word is as true today as it was in 1976.

These days, in our multi-channel, text-messaging, cyberspace existence, the ideas we receive and pump out tend to be a little more stripped down and immediate. A couple of years back, campaigning group Cymuned, famous for their slogan of *Dal Dy Dir!* (Hold your ground!), produced a couple of matching posters that seemed to me to sum up the situation beautifully, at least as far as the Welsh language was concerned, in the areas where it was still strong. The two posters sat side by side: the English one was a simple exhortation: Learn Our Language; the Welsh one said, *Helpwch y Dysgwyr* (Help the learners); six words that more or less say it all.

Despite the avalanche of incomers moving into Wales (about 25% of the population were born outside Wales, far, far higher than any other country in the UK), there's a strange thing going on with our national perspective. Whether it's the Assembly, or the rugby, or the Manics, or Charlotte Church, who knows, but there is a consistently high – and growing – proportion of people in Wales who identify first as Welsh, before British or European. This seems to include a great many people who have moved here from elsewhere, and that's deeply encouraging. As England struggles with its post-imperial identity, Wales, it seems to me, has the best chance ever of losing its shackles, its centuries of lacerating self-doubt, and working out, *on its own terms*, precisely what and how it wants to be in the future. It will take tough choices, but it could reap huge rewards.

Just shouting 'Wales!' and 'Welsh!' at everything is not enough, and those who do so should be avoided like the plague. As Professor R R Davies, in his 1992 address to the

Cymmorodion Society, put it: 'Welshness should be lived, not protested; experienced, not raucously proclaimed. Our distrust is immediately triggered by those who protest their Welshness, not least because it is usually a preface to a bout of sentimentality, a poor argument, or a shifty political or moral decision.'

To see it the Welsh way requires, for an English person, a whole new panorama. The British mindset, the one in which we English have been raised, is addicted to power and strength and size: it has not yet recovered from the speedy loss of Empire and all that went with it. All British Prime Ministers have to suck up to whoever is in the White House, desperate to maintain that special relationship that we hear so much about, but that most Americans have never heard of. All British politicians have to defend frankly indefensible vestiges of our macho past, from the permanent seat on the UN Security Council to ritual jingoistic posturing against our near neighbours. To accept the Welsh scale of things as being not just normal, but desirable, requires the acceptance that small is good, is inherently valuable in itself, and can take us to new, more exciting and interesting places that chest-beating and shouting cannot.

As the world moves on, and America's status as sole superpower melts in the heat of growing Chinese and Indian potency, do we want to stay hitched to a largely spent force, one that is itself tacked on to another that is also rapidly waning? I'd say not. I'd also suggest that a re-alignment of power between the cultures and countries of these islands could reap huge benefits for us all. The potential – for both Wales and England – to end the period of our being each others' neighbours from hell is tantalisingly close.

Chapter 7

IN THE BEGINNING:
A Brief Early History

We can trace almost all the disasters of English history to the influence of Wales.

Evelyn Waugh, *Decline and Fall*, 1928

The bulk of the cross-border sniping that we discussed in this book has come from the past few hundred years. English antipathy towards the Welsh, however, goes back an awful lot further to times when the concepts of 'England' and 'Wales' had barely come into existence. This is a very long game. Wales, as we recognise it, can be dated to around 500 BC, when the island of Britain was first settled by the Celts, who probably migrated here from their base in mid Europe. The Celts brought their druidic faith, their intricate artwork and their language, which eventually mutated into two branches, one (known as Brythonic) being the recognisable forerunner of the Welsh, Cornish and Breton tongues, the other (Godeilic) producing Manx and Scots and Irish Gaelic. The arrival of the Romans in 43AD changed everything. Most parts of what we now know as England became thoroughly Romanised, with the Celtic tribes of the north and west proving to be a far harder nut to crack. That the tribes of Wales proved to be such a challenge to the Romans is evident from the fact that two of their three great legionary garrison cities were on the Welsh border, at Chester (Deva) and Caerleon (Isca).

Alfred the great finally finds a way to unite all the tribes of England.

It was during the Roman occupation that Wales first began to swim into view as a discrete entity, a process that continued apace following the Romans' departure in the fourth century. The period between the end of the Roman occupation and the arrival of the Normans in 1066 has traditionally been known by the catch-all phrase: the Dark Ages, as if nothing much happened and the people of these islands retreated into a stunted barbarism. During these centuries, the native British Celts were gradually pushed into the areas of northern and western Britain by successive waves of invaders, particularly Angles, Saxons and Jutes. Thus, the three countries of England, Wales and Scotland began to form.

If – and it's a big if – this period could be described as the

Dark Ages for England, it most certainly could not for Wales. Indeed, the period after the Romans was something of a golden age here, with Wales at the centre of an international European network of trade and pilgrimage based on sea travel, and there was an upsurge in religious devotion and education. But, already, in the kingdoms of England, mutterings against the Welsh were growing. Bede, the historian monk from Northumbria, wrote in his *Ecclesiastical History of the English People* (c.730 AD):

> *The Britons [i.e. the Brythons or Welsh], though they, for the most part, through innate hatred, are adverse to the English nation, and wrongfully, and from wicked custom, oppose the appointed Easter of the whole Catholic Church; yet, from both the Divine and human power withstanding them, can in no way prevail as they desire; for though in part they are their own masters yet elsewhere they are also brought under subjection to the English.*

It was a variation on a theme that many have returned to over the ensuing thirteen centuries. The best-known relic of English-Welsh animosity from this time is Offa's Dyke, built in the latter half of the eighth century, to demarcate the lands of the Welsh princes from those of Offa, king of Mercia (an area roughly corresponding to the English Midlands). It's been a thoroughly effective mark on the landscape: the England-Wales border has more or less followed the line of the Dyke ever since.

In the tenth century, the early Wales was a loose confederation (with occasional in-bickering) of autonomous provinces, areas that also largely corresponded to modern boundaries. Under the leadership of, first, Rhodri Mawr and, then, his grandson, Hywel Dda (Hywel the Good), king of Deheubarth (south-west Wales or the former Dyfed), the fractious kingdoms became united, in a process that was repeated by subsequent rulers over the coming few centuries. The Norman invasion of 1066 had little immediate effect in most of Wales, although inroads were gradually made into the more fertile, productive lands of the south. The kingdoms of Powys and, especially, Gwynedd became the bastions of Welsh survival. By the mid thirteenth century, astute politicking and some brute force had produced an unprecedented, unified Wales under the rule of Gwynedd's Llywelyn ap Gruffudd. But everything was about to change.

The military campaign of the English king Edward I (1239-1307, king from 1272) was the only instance I can recall of Wales even being mentioned in my school history lessons. Growing up in Worcestershire, just forty or so miles from the Welsh border, this lack of teaching about our very near neighbour was sadly not surprising; neither was the tone, which I can so clearly remember, of our sour-faced history teacher, droning on about Edward having to quell the rebellious Welsh and teach them a lesson. There was no instruction in any of the historical background to Edward's war, his brutal suppression of Welsh leaders, nor his imposition of an alien system of law on a country with its own very distinct (and far fairer) legal traditions.

For Edward's war against the Welsh was truly brutal – as well as peevish. The new king was furious at the refusal of the Prince of Wales, Llywelyn ap Gruffudd, the grandson of Llywelyn Fawr, to appear in London, in order to pay homage to him. Llywelyn's reason for this snub is hard to establish, although the fact that his wife Elinor had been captured at sea and imprisoned in Windsor was, perhaps, enough to make him feel deeply – and understandably – suspicious of a trip to London. Not that Edward I saw it that way. Llywelyn's non-appearance was just the spark he was waiting for. Llywelyn wrote to Edward three times, indicating that he was willing to

' WE'LL DO WITHOUT THE LEYLANDII OFFA. '

Original Cartoon: Toby Driver

mediate, with the King of France as a willing go-between, but Edward ignored the correspondence and declared Llywelyn a rebel and the Welsh an enemy. Tens of thousands of troops were sent west, Marcher Lords were encouraged to grab any land they could, and Edward began to build the mighty chain of fortresses that remain as the most potent symbols of this brutal time.

Edward's belligerence brought English anti-Welshness to new heights and changed the balance of power for ever. When Llywelyn was killed, in December 1282, Edward knew that he could henceforth ride roughshod over the traditions and tribes of Wales, and he wasted no time in doing just that. His new castles, and their accompanying bastide towns, became English-only enclaves, where Welsh people had no rights whatsoever. At Flint, for example, site of the first of Edward's so-called iron ring of castles, the town's initial charter of 1284 decreed that no Welshman was 'allowed to hold civic office, carry weapons, hold assemblies or to purchase land or property in the borough,' while the English settlers could, 'gather wood in the woods of the Welsh without payment.' Three more charters, granted in the following century, tightened the thumbscrews on the native Welsh even further. The Welsh – no surprise – resented being treated so harshly in their own land, and started to resist the worst of the settlers' arrogance. The stand-off culminated in a petition being sent by the English burgesses of the borough to the king, in 1395: it complained of 'the ill-will of the Welsh and their trouble-making and defiance of the law.' It was like a bunch of spoilt brat bullies, whining to teacher when their victim finally hits back.

Edward's imposition of a system of English boroughs – such as those at Denbigh, Rhuddlan, Caernarfon, Conwy, Flint and Beaumaris, in the deepest parts of Cymru Gymraeg, was little more than an early and vicious form of apartheid. In each and every one, rules against the locals were many and punitive, and it is hardly surprising that antagonism broke out between the two sides. These were not battles between equals, however. Whereas the Welsh had only their cunning, and their loyalty to each other and their land to fall back on, the English residents had the full might of medieval law on their side, and they never missed a chance to activate it. It is small wonder that Welsh resentment simmered throughout the fourteenth century, culminating in the ultimately unsuccessful rebellion of Owain Glyndŵr, when the hope of a free and fair Wales briefly sparkled.

Glyndŵr's uprising, hardly surprisingly, sparked a raft of new controls against the Welsh. In Chester, a local bye-law decreed that no Welshman should be allowed to stay in the city after dark, 'on pain of decapitation.' A similar law, in another border city, Hereford, made it permissible to kill a Welshman, but only with a longbow, on a Sunday and in the Cathedral Close! On a national level, the English parliament introduced a succession of harsh Penal Codes that restricted the rights of Welsh people, even in Wales. The 1401 *Rotuli Parliamentorum* decreed that, 'it is ordained... that no Englishman shall be convicted by any Welshman within the land of Wales. It is ordained that... from henceforth no Welshman shall be armed nor bear defensible armour... nor shall be put into any office in Wales or the Marches.' This last point, banning any Welshman from public office (including in the church), was ruthlessly enforced, as was seen in 1433, when the Deputy Justice in southern Wales, John Scudamore, was sacked because he was married to a Welsh woman.

Anti-Welsh sentiment was not restricted only to Wales. Such was the prevailing atmosphere of the day, that it was a tough time to be Welsh in England. Numerous tales of attacks on Welsh merchants and stockmen in London and elsewhere survive from this time. There were anti-Welsh riots in Oxford, where crowds were recorded as baying, 'Slay the Welsh dogs and their whelps.' In the same city, Welsh students at the University were forced to piss on the town gates and then kiss the spot.

The fifteenth century saw the rise to the English throne of the Tudor dynasty, with its many Welsh connections. Some of the punitive restrictions against land ownership and civic office were relaxed, and, indeed, a few Welshmen were promoted to high positions within the London Court. Ultimately, however, the Tudors only cemented the Welsh in with the English, leading to the inevitable Act of Union under King Henry VIII, in 1536. It's a misleading title, and one that was not used to describe the

Act until the twentieth century, for it implies a certain level of equality between the two nations, when there was, in reality, anything but. Calling it an Act of Union suggests parity with the Acts of 1707 and 1800 that brought Scotland and Ireland into the Union. But those were the results of decisions of independent parliaments in Edinburgh, Dublin and London to merge their identity. There was no such process afoot in Wales. The so-called Act of Union was a unilateral decision by Westminster, a parliament that believed it spoke for Wales, although it had absolutely no Welsh representation in it at the time.

The 1536 Act was unambiguous in its intent and scope. It states that, 'His Highness... hath ordained, enacted and established that his said country or dominion of Wales shall stand and continue for ever from henceforth incorporated, united and annexed to and with his Realm of England.' The Act also decreed that English was to be the only language of the courts and other official bodies in Wales, even at a time when the majority of the population had little or no English. This created a two-tier Wales, comprising English-speaking lords and masters and a Welsh-speaking proletariat. In many ways, this period set in stone the struggles and the injustices that we are still trying to redress, nearly five hundred years later.

Even in the darkest times of anti-Welsh sentiment, before 1536, there was a certain tacit acceptance that the Welsh legal system was sufficient in its tradition and scope to serve Welsh-speaking Wales. This was a very different system from the one practised in England. Welsh medieval law was based on common sense, recompense and reconciliation, in stark contrast to the English laws, which were deeply hierarchical, and often bloody and violent in their pursuit of revenge. The Welsh laws were codified and recorded, in a huge exercise at Hendy-gwyn-ar-Daf (Whitland) Carmarthenshire, in 930 AD. Nearly eleven hundred years later, many of these laws are still breathtaking in their apparent modernity and compassion. Women, for example, were allowed to initiate divorce proceedings (adultery, and even bad breath, were some of the permissible reasons), could inherit and own property (something not introduced into English law until 1883) and were granted the right to compensation if beaten by their husbands. Bastard children were given full parity with legitimate offspring, medical treatment was legally available (and mostly free) to all, and theft (of food) was unpunished if it was to keep people alive. This last law is in painful contrast to the long, grim list of starving men, women and children who were executed in Wales and England, under English law, until as late as the nineteenth century, for crimes such as stealing a lamb, or even a loaf of bread.

All this admirable legal framework was demolished with the Acts of Union, in the first half of the sixteenth century: the crucial clause in the 1536 Act stated that, 'The laws, ordinances and statutes of this realm of England forever, and none other laws... shall be... used in... Wales.' In practice, many Welsh people still continued unofficially to operate *Cyfraith Hywel* (the Law of Hywel, so-called after Hywel Dda, the King of Deheubarth, who instigated the codifying and recording of the Welsh laws), even if there was no longer any legal basis in it. Even today, the laws of Hywel Dda, after more than a millennium, seem thorough, robust and, most importantly, *fair*. Not for nothing has English (and other) law moved steadily in its direction, albeit painfully slowly, and with much bloodshed and anguish en route.

When a country loses its capacity to make its own laws, it loses much of its identity as a nation. Even when Scotland was appropriated into Great Britain and, then, the United Kingdom, the separate Scottish legal system was kept intact, and remains so to this day. This has undoubtedly kept Scottish identity more contained and visible in a way that was long denied to Wales. A modern updating of *Cyfraith Hywel* would be an inspirational basis for a sophisticated and tolerant legal framework in Wales. The bad breath clause in particular....

All conquered people are suspicious of their conquerors. The English have forgotten that they have conquered the Welsh, but some ages will elapse before the Welsh forget that the English have conquered them.

George Borrow, *Wild Wales*, 1862

The Welsh are a conquered race, and have very little regard for their conquerors, and even some of the most ignorant of them are so stupid as to entertain the notion of reclaiming their country from the English.

H. L. Spring, *Lady Cambria*, 1867

Postscript

My Journey to Wales

I'm a firm believer in the idea that we can just as readily fall in love with places as with people. Sometimes, it's a passionate burst, love at first sight, or the odd dirty weekend. And sometimes, it's a growing, deepening affair of the heart that matures into a lifelong commitment.

Wales hooked me at a very early age. Growing up in Kidderminster, north Worcestershire, meant that A E Housman's 'blue remembered hills' of the borders were my exotic western horizon – a good deal more exotic, it should be remembered, than if you looked the other way and saw the Black Country and Brum smouldering into the distance. A red dragon kite, bought at a border village fete when I was about five, became my most treasured possession and caused months of tantrums when it was lost in a house move. Soon after, I started my lifelong addiction to collecting maps. Hours were spent poring over purple Ordnance Surveys of Wales, rolling the other-worldly names over my tongue and stroking the savage contours with relish. By the age of eleven, I'd found a *Teach Yourself Welsh* book in a jumble sale, and was busily attempting to get past *rydw i'n hoffi coffi*, a statement I couldn't make without giggling. And still can't, to be honest.

When it came to choosing a university, I dabbled with the idea of going to Wales, but there were more pressing needs for a hormonally-challenged eighteen-year-old, struggling with his sexuality. Going to university in London gave me the chance not so much to come out of the closet, but to burst out of it with such gusto that the door fell off its hinges, never to be shut again. What a hell of a relief! After doing a sabbatical year as student union president in my college, I somehow got elected as an independent to the National Union of Students' executive. This was 1988, and the NUS was being run by a Kinnockite cabal of Labour Students, with the opposition provided by a potpourri of Trotskyite paper-sellers. I shared an office for a few months with one of the very few other independent executive members, one Lembit Öpik, who hadn't yet come out as a Liberal. He made an unsuccessful bid for the presidency of the NUS, under the slogan *Like it? You'll Lembit!* You'll go far, I thought. Little over a decade later, he was my MP. Scary.

The work on NUS allowed me to get involved with the Welsh arm of the movement, UCMC (Undeb Cenedlaethol Myfyrwyr Cymru), which most people in the London HQ verbally abbreviated to 'yekker-mek'. I went to a few UCMC conferences, where I gravitated towards the Plaid Cymru activists, for the very simple reason that they were a great deal more interesting, and more fun to be with, than the shiny-eyed little careerists of the Labour party. The best part of twenty years later, it's an opinion I've barely altered at all. The main reason I've become a member of Plaid since living in Wales is because of the type of people it attracts. The vast majority of Plaidwyr that I've come across have been courteous, thoughtful, erudite, passionate and absolutely committed to improving the lot of their country and the world beyond it. A crucial point here is that true "nationalism" is firmly internationalist in its outlook, and Plaid, and many of its stalwarts, have an exemplary record in this regard. By contrast, the vast majority of Labour activists that I've met in Wales have been shifty political anoraks, whose commitment is only to furthering their own career or destroying someone else's – often at the same stroke.

Having failed to move to Wales for university, I then managed not to do it again. A couple of years in office-bound voluntary sector jobs made me quickly realise that I was a useless employee, and should really be out there, trying to do my own thing, whatever that was. While in a job in Cambridge (by far the worst place I have ever lived; the embodiment of all that is aggressive and clenched about Middle England), I'd managed to get a publisher interested in putting out two youth-oriented guide books that I'd written, to Birmingham and Manchester. Although they were published to yawning indifference, I decided that it was high time to be making my way as a freelance writer. Again, I pondered where to live. Wales appealed, very much indeed, but Birmingham, the city in which I was born and which provided much of the backdrop to my upbringing, got in first. It was a kind of *hiraeth* that I needed to work through; to get to know my own back yard all over again and from a new angle, to write about and from the place that spawned me. So, in summer 1991, I chucked the job in Cambridge, spent a couple of months travelling around Ireland, and then set myself up on the Enterprise Allowance Scheme (forty quid a week and a born-again Christian Business Adviser who would fondle my knee during advice sessions) as Birmingham's newest freelancer.

Without doubt, and despite the flashy new Selfridges and legion of Fun Bars that have sprung up recently, Birmingham remains the UK's comedy city. It's the easiest place to take the piss out of, and often for good reason. The accent, Spaghetti Junction, a cultural pedigree of *Crossroads* and Ozzy Osbourne, and a reputation as a 1970s backwater have all come to symbolise the second city, despite its grand pretensions. If you want Brum in a nutshell, it's the city that bid for the Olympics, and ended up instead with the Eurovision Song Contest.

Living in the city that's the butt-end of every joke produces a strange attitude in its inhabitants. One of the things I love about Birmingham is its self-deprecating sense of humour, its sheer inability, unlike, say, Manchester, Newcastle or Glasgow, to take itself too seriously. For a few years, I was on the board of directors of the city's annual literature festival. One year, we flew in an eminent American writer for a series of events. At Birmingham Airport, he found a taxi and settled happily in the back. 'Gee,' he enthused to the taxi driver, 'd'you know, I've never been to Birmingham before.' The taxi driver eyed him warily in his rear-view mirror, before laconically replying, in a broad Brum accent, 'Well, yow ain't missed mooch, then, 'ave yow?'

This attitude seeps into all areas of Brum life. Ask anyone who lives there what's so good about it and you'll almost always get the answer, 'It's so easy to get to anywhere else from there.' In other words, the best thing about being there is that you can be somewhere else, anywhere else, really, very quickly. London, Manchester, Sheffield, Bristol, the Peak District and the Cotswolds are all within a couple of hours. As is Wales: a fact that sustained me greatly throughout my nine years in Brum. Countless weekends would find me heading west, breathing a huge sigh of relief as I passed the *Croeso i Gymru* sign and clocked the first *Teleffon* box.

Having written those two books, about Birmingham and Manchester (a further two, on Bristol/Bath and Glasgow were due to come out, when the publishers, Harrap, went down the corporate toilet, taking my little series with them), I was invited down to talk with the Rough Guides. This was when they were still sparky, independent and idealistic, and based in a shambolic house in suburban south London. They were, they told me, planning to produce books on Britain for the first time. As someone with a bit of a track record in domestic travel writing aimed at younger people, would I be interested in contributing? I was. Very.

Being based in the English Midlands, it seemed natural for me to take on that area, but I was also keen to spend more time in Wales and get to know it better, so I put in an early request to write the Wales book. The only thing was that they weren't planning a Wales book. Scotland was to get its own volume, but Wales was due to be apportioned a whole two chapters appended on to the England tome. England'n'Wales: same old story. Being a trendy, liberal, London publisher seemed to be no barrier to being just as pompous and patronising as ever towards Cymru.

In the first planning meeting, I argued loudly for a separate Wales volume. One of the Rough Guide directors grew red-faced and furious, and ended up thumping the table as he ranted, 'But who the fuck is going to buy a book about *Wales*?' He spat the name out as if it was a particularly unpalatable bit of gristle. I didn't budge and continued to argue that the three British countries warranted three separate books. Eventually, and after many weeks of aggro, my stubbornness won out.

To research that first *Rough Guide to Wales*, I spent most of the spring and summer of 1992 ambling happily around the country, with a hire car and a tent. Having a good reason to poke around old churches and dusty civic museums was a fabulous motivation, not that you really need a reason to be nosy in Wales. People were astonishingly helpful. I lost count of the number of times I was invited for supper, or plied with beer in remote pubs, just because I was showing an interest. It was like an enormous treasure hunt: one enquiry would lead on to someone else's phone number, who'd recommend a friend or relative somewhere else, who'd take me to a party and introduce me to a whole load of new people, all with such a depth of knowledge and enthusiasm for their *milltir sgwar* to share.

The *Rough Guide* needed updating every three years, but it also gave me a stack of new friends and acquaintances, so that I found myself coming more and more across the border for short holidays and a social life. By the mid 1990s, the free party scene was erupting everywhere, and I was spending numerous weekends dancing glazed-eyed in remote Welsh forests, quarries and beaches. The quick-fired lust was deepening into a fully-fledged love, one that was proving harder and harder to resist on a permanent basis. I'd pulled back from moving to Wales to go to university, and again, when I became freelance. But it was a force that could be resisted no longer.

Therapy-speak will tell you that it is the making of the decision that is the tough bit. Once that's done, all else is supposed to flow effortlessly in the direction of a decision well made. Not in this case. When I finally, firmly decided to move to Wales, I seemed to become the epicentre of a maelstrom: my world turned upside down as obstacles and objections rained down. Never before, or since, have I lived through a period of such chaos. Not a day went by without someone telling me I was mad, I'd last ten minutes, I'd be lynched on arrival in Llareggub, at the very least I was condemning myself to a boyfriend-less life of Trappist solitude. Only a handful of true friends knew me well enough to know that this was something I had to do and was always going to do, at some point. The reaction of the crowd down the pub, the pack I partied with and my fellow arts and media whores was almost violent in its condemnation. But it wasn't enough to change my mind. Extreme stubbornness can have its advantages.

The decision wasn't a moment of great epiphany. No alarums

sounded, no clouds parted; a switch somewhere deep inside me flicked quietly from OFF to ON, and I was away. The switch flicked as I and a close friend shared a week in a rented cottage in Abergynolwyn, at the time of the Spring Equinox in the year 2000. A small fit of millennial blood-rush was coursing through my veins; recent access to the internet had shown me how portable the life of a freelance writer could be; the creative doors, on which I'd been repeatedly knocking in the Midlands, remained obstinately shut. All factors pointed to change, well, all factors except one.

At that time, my grandmother, known as Bom Bom, a woman who'd been the major motherly force in my often wayward life, was confined to a nursing home in Leamington Spa, twenty miles down the road from where I lived in southern Birmingham. She was as miserable as hell in there, and visiting her most weeks, I could see the life draining out of her hunched frame. Her spirit was dying, her body was dying, her will to live was dying, but her mind was as clear, wise and sparky as ever. It's an evil combination.

I returned from Abergynolwyn that Easter, immediately gave notice on my rented Birmingham house, and started looking for a place to live in Wales. Bom Bom was uppermost in my mind. Telling her that I was to follow my dream and move to the place that I'd wanted to be ever since I could remember was something I knew that she would instinctively understand and support. But, for her, the only tangible result would be that she would see me very much less frequently. Those days, for her, were a long, living nightmare and I knew all too well how much visits from me or my sister meant to her, and to us. As physical life ebbed slowly away, her passion for sharing with us her truths, and hearing ours, became ever stronger. We had some of our best conversations ever in that awful place that stank of pee and loneliness – or rather, in the gardens, where we'd sit and share a cracked cup of lukewarm tea and a Silk Cut. If I went to Wales all that would go.

Also approaching was the tenth anniversary of the death of Dan Dan, my granddad and Bom Bom's late husband (Dan Dan, incidentally, is the name that Tony Benn's grandchildren call him. I remember the horror with which my Dan Dan, a natural Tory of the old school, discovered that. I finally understood how the revelation felt for him, when I discovered the truly terrifying fact that Michael Barrymore's real name is Michael Parker). Bom Bom and Dan Dan had been together since teenage years in Beverley, in the East Riding of Yorkshire. Had Yorkshire grammar schools in the 1920s been like American high schools of the 1950s, BB and DD would doubtless have appeared in the Yearbook as the Couple Most Likely To Make It. They were a dashing pair, who embarked on a lifelong adventure of which they never tired.

The anniversary of Dan Dan's death proved to be the day when I finally told her of my plan. I'd found a wee flat between Aberystwyth and Machynlleth, and was moving in within the month. I bought a bunch of lilies on the way to the nursing home. They're flowers I never normally buy, but this was a day to remember death and its place in life, so they seemed fitting. Bom Bom was not herself, not even her much reduced self, that day. She'd wanted to make it to the year 2000, but that had been the last of her ambitions, and now, four months into the new millennium, there was nothing left. She'd been rightly proud of how well she'd managed her life and affairs in the ten years since losing Dan Dan, but a decade of that was up now, and maybe that was enough. On my last visit, I'd chickened out of telling her of my intentions (kidding myself that as I hadn't actually got a forwarding address yet, I might not be going, so best not upset an old lady... and so on). Seeing how deflated and defeated she seemed already, the icy water of cowardice started to flow through me again. But I had to tell her.

We talked about Dan Dan for an hour, before fresh tea was ordered and delivered. I knew it was the moment. 'Erm, I've got some rather big news...' I mumbled. Bom Bom visibly brightened and turned, smiling, towards me. 'Have you?' she said in a voice of a strength and clarity I hadn't heard for months. Before I'd even managed to get out another word, she said, 'So, are you moving to the land of your fathers at last? At long last.' She smiled. I think I cried. I think she did, too. I was so surprised and delighted by her response that I forgot to ask what her question had actually meant. Was it just a figure of speech? Or were there some drops of Welsh blood coursing through our veins from way back when?

There never was another chance to ask. The next time I saw her was a week later, by which time she'd fallen into a coma. Life was draining steadily out of her, but even with almost no faculties remaining, she waited until my sister and I had arrived from Birmingham, my mum from Paris, and we'd all had time to say our goodbyes to her and helloes to each other, before she finally breathed her last. Seeing someone you love die in peace is one of the most beautiful things you can possibly witness, especially when they choose their moment with such exquisite precision. She died at 5am on a beautiful May morning, with the streets quiet and sun rising.

Within ten days, I was a resident of Llangynfelyn, a wee speck of a place, between mountain and sea, in northern Ceredigion. It had taken thirty-three years, but I was finally a citizen of Cymru.

The Author

At the age of eleven, Mike Parker bought himself a *Teach Yourself Welsh* book and was hooked. Growing up in north Worcestershire, the 'blue remembered hills' of the Borders were his western horizon, and he took every opportunity to head over Offa's Dyke. Since he started shaving, he has written books on four UK cities, the gay scenes of Scotland, Ireland and northern England, and has been the co-author of all five editions of the best-selling *Rough Guide to Wales*. Alongside the travel writing, he has dabbled in careers as useless as stand-up comedy and TV presenting.

His work on the *Rough Guide* necessitated spending increasing amounts of time in Wales and in early 2000, in a fit of millennial bloodrush to the head, he decided finally to move to rural mid Wales. He wrote and presented a one-off St David's Day special for ITV Wales in 2002, which resulted in him being commissioned to write and present two series of *Coast to Coast*, where Mike took twelve journeys in different boats around the Welsh coast. This emphatically made him realise that he was no sailor, and he's since returned to dry land to make three series of the highly popular *Great Welsh Roads*, which sees Mike and his dog Patsy tour the country in his camper van. He is now living with his partner Peredur near Machynlleth.

For a full list of our Welsh-interest
books, send now for a free copy of our
catalogue, or why not surf into our fully
updated website where you may buy
books and other items on-line:

www.ylolfa.com

Y Lolfa, Talybont, Ceredigion, Cymru SY24 5HE
www.ylolfa.com
ylolfa@ylolfa.com
ffôn 01970 832 304
ffacs 01970 832 718